I0759555

SIMPLY DONABE

SIMPLY DONABE

Naoko Takei Moore

JAPANESE ONE-POT RECIPES

INTRODUCTION

Donabe is a Way of Life

Donabe cooking is my simple joy – it shapes my lifestyle.

The donabe, a Japanese clay pot, has been a staple in Japanese cuisine and culture for centuries. The word consists of two characters: 土 (*do*) meaning 'clay', and 鍋 (*nabe*) meaning 'pot'. Almost every household in Japan owns at least one donabe, often used for cosy hotpot dishes during cold seasons. Donabe are also loved by professional chefs for their efficiency and aesthetic beauty, and are used widely in both traditional and modern restaurants across Japan. But a donabe is so much more than just a cooking vessel – it's a way of life that extends beyond recipes.

Embracing the donabe way involves a deep appreciation for the process of preparing and sharing meals with intention. Donabe cooking plays a pivotal role in bringing people together – whether at home or in an izakaya, gathering around a donabe, setting up ingredients, cooking and sharing from the same pot creates lasting memories. When the lid is lifted to reveal the finished dish, all eyes focus on the donabe. There's a moment of anticipation, a held breath and then a collective 'wow' of excitement. There is something truly magical about the donabe experience – not just the food itself, but the shared joy of the process and how it brings people together.

But a donabe doesn't always have to be cooked and shared with others. It has also become my personal ritual, a quiet moment of connection between myself and the ingredients. I often cherish cooking with a donabe alone, letting the gentle simmering sound and rising steam turn my kitchen into a peaceful space. Cooking with a donabe grounds me, helping me pay more attention to each ingredient and each step. It's therapeutic and inspires me to become creative at the same time. This way of cooking brings a natural rhythm to my day and a sense of satisfaction in preparing each meal with care.

Growing up in Tokyo, I was fortunate to enjoy my mom's delicious cooking every day and learned from her. She was such an amazing cook and taught me how to cook from a young age. Some of my earliest cooking memories include making onigiri, tamago sando, rolling mochi, shaving katsuobushi and preparing yose-nabe hotpot by adding ready-prepared ingredients to the donabe for the family. She passed away in 2016, and I miss her and her cooking dearly, but her love and comforting culinary style live on in me.

I moved to Los Angeles in 2001. Soon after, my passion for sharing Japanese home cooking with people in the US grew. I realised that donabe – both my beloved cookware and way of cooking – was something I truly wanted to introduce. This realisation coincided with a moment when I tasted incredible rice cooked in a donabe crafted by Nagatani-en, an eighth-generation kiln from Iga, Japan. In 2008, I started TOIRO, my own business importing and selling authentic Iga-yaki (Iga-style) donabe from Nagatani-en, while also hosting donabe cooking classes in my small home kitchen.

At the time, donabe cooking was practically unknown outside of Japanese and Asian cultures, and introducing it was a big challenge. I even had to start by teaching people how to pronounce it: it's doh-nah-bay, not doh-nah-bee! But through grassroots efforts, more and more people began to discover and appreciate donabe cooking. In 2015, I co-authored a cookbook, *DONABE: Classic and Modern Japanese Clay Pot Cooking* (Ten Speed Press), helping to spread the joy of donabe even further. My business continued to grow, and in 2017 I opened a brick-and-mortar shop in West Hollywood. Now, I curate a wide selection of artisan donabe, kitchenware, tableware and food items from all over Japan – all to share a way of living through donabe cooking and Japanese food culture, with people around the world.

Seeing how far donabe cooking has come since I first started promoting it is deeply rewarding. Back then, a donabe was rarely recognised outside of Japan and was usually referred to as a 'Japanese clay pot' or 'Japanese earthenware'. But today, I am so proud to see donabe introduced by its rightful name in many publications (just like wasabi is now wasabi, not 'Japanese horseradish'). This achievement feels deeply personal and means so much to me.

I believe donabe cooking continues to grow in popularity because it's so flexible and accommodating – you can easily create a stress-free and delicious one-pot dish. It's not about special technique; it's about the experience. And beyond convenience, a donabe brings something even more special to the table.

Life is short and every meal counts. I often think about how many more meals I will have in my lifetime – each one holds meaning in its own way. Whether you are preparing a feast or a simple one-pot meal with your donabe, it's always *ichigo ichie* – every moment happens once in a lifetime. That's the magic of donabe, and I can't wait to share it with you!

NAOKO TAKEI MOORE
(from home in LA)

I

WELCOME TO HAPPY DONABE LIFE

Cooking with a Donabe

A donabe is an earthenware pot that has been used in Japanese cooking for centuries. In fact, its origins are said to date back more than 10,000 years ago to the Jomon period in Japan.

MY LOVE FOR IGA-YAKI DONABE

Today, donabe are made by many different producers, both traditional and modern, across Japan. There is also a wide range in quality – from inexpensive, mass-produced donabe to high-end, hand-thrown artisan pieces. But among them, Iga-yaki donabe from Iga, Japan, stand out as some of the most historic and highly regarded. And that's the donabe of my choice. In fact, I have a few dozen Iga-yaki donabe in different sizes, designs and for different purposes that I regularly use! Iga has a 1,300-year-plus history of pottery making, and its donabe, crafted from the region's unique local clay, are known to be among the most durable and heat-resistant earthenware in the world. Iga clay comes from an area that was once the bed of ancient Lake Biwa, around 4 million years ago. The prehistoric fossilised microorganisms in the clay create a porous texture when fired, giving Iga-yaki donabe remarkable heat-retention abilities.

HOW DONABE ENHANCE COOKING

One of the key benefits of cooking with a donabe is its ability to absorb and retain heat, gradually building temperature and cooling down slowly after the heat is turned off. In fact, the contents tend to stay hot for an extended period of time through residual heat. This steady heating and slow cooling process helps ingredients develop deeper layers of flavour, making it ideal for stews, braised dishes and even rice.

Iga-yaki donabe excel in this, due to their exceptional high heat-retention ability and porous clay body. Iga clay is a particularly coarse clay, which literally breathes during cooking and promotes the ideal heat distribution. Even if you are not using an Iga-yaki donabe, a well-made donabe will offer similar benefits – allowing for gentle, even cooking that naturally enhances umami.

Additionally, the pot's glaze naturally promotes 'far infrared' radiation when heated – similar to how glowing charcoal cooks food without direct flame. This allows donabe to generate a steady, penetrating heat that cooks ingredients evenly while sealing in moisture and drawing out their natural flavours. I always feel that food tastes better when cooked in a donabe, even with minimal seasoning or effort. That's why I often tell people: 'Let the donabe do the work for you!'

A DONABE FOR A LIFETIME

Beyond its cooking benefits, a high-quality donabe (like an Iga-yaki donabe) can last for many years. Some of my donabe are already more than 15 years old and frequently used, yet they continue to perform beautifully. Over time, as you cook with a donabe, it develops a natural patina and also some tiny chipped parts here and there, adding character and making it more personal – something to cherish. Cooking and serving with a donabe brings warmth to the table.

Each time I cook with mine, I feel a connection to the earth, history and tradition behind it. That's the magic of the donabe – it's not just cookware; it's an experience.

How to Choose your Donabe

At my shop, TOIRO, one of the most common questions we receive from new customers is: 'Which donabe do you recommend for someone new to donabe cooking?' or 'If I need just one donabe, what should it be?' Over centuries, the art of donabe has evolved, and today, there are many different styles and types, crafted by artisans across Japan. With so many options, it can feel overwhelming to choose the right one. So, here is my guide to help you select a donabe that can become a staple in your everyday cooking.

CHOOSING BY FUNCTION

These are the types of donabe I use most frequently, and they are also used in this book. The classic-style donabe is the most basic type, and many other specialised donabe share its core functions while offering additional features or excelling in specific cooking methods.

CLASSIC-STYLE DONABE: This is the most traditional and standard type of donabe, consisting of a bowl and a lid. It's great for any dish you would cook in a pot, including hotpot, soup, stew, braising and rice. If you are looking for a donabe that covers all the basic functions, or if you are not sure which donabe to pick for your first one, I highly recommend a classic-style donabe. Even if you plan to own multiple donabe at home, having at least one classic-style donabe is always a good idea – it's an essential in my kitchen. Most of the donabe recipes in this book can be made using this.

DONABE FOR SOUPS, STEWS AND BRAISING (CLASSIC-STYLE WITH EXTRA-THICK BODY): If you are looking for a donabe with enhanced heat retention or one that excels in slow cooking, choose a donabe with an extra-thick body. The thick, porous clay absorbs heat more gradually than a regular classic-style donabe and retains it for a longer period. This means your soup stays hot in the donabe, so you don't have to worry about reheating when you want a second serving! The extra-thick body makes it ideal for long, slow cooking – whether you are braising on the stovetop or in the oven for hours. This type of donabe is also excellent for cooking beans from scratch, as the sustained, steady heat helps soften them evenly. Some styles come with a sturdy, tight-sealing lid, which creates stronger pressure during cooking compared to a regular donabe lid, making it ideal for waterless cooking. This method uses the natural moisture released by ingredients instead of added liquid, intensifying flavours while keeping the texture tender and juicy. And, of course, this donabe can be used for cooking anything you would cook in a regular classic-style donabe.

DONABE RICE COOKER: This donabe is designed to cook rice efficiently and with ease. While a classic-style donabe can also make excellent rice, it requires some skill to get it just right – you need to know when to adjust the heat, watch for boil-overs and manage timing carefully. Today, many producers offer specialised donabe for rice cooking, designed to simplify the process while still producing delicious, fluffy rice. Donabe rice cookers are also versatile enough to function as a classic-style donabe, making them a great option for everyday use.

DONABE STEAMER: This style of donabe comes with a steam grate, allowing for effective steaming – ranging from gentle, slow cooking to high-intensity steaming. With the 'far infrared' radiation effect generated by the donabe, ingredients can cook faster while maintaining their ideal texture, especially vegetables. This is a great donabe for someone who wants to cook flavourful dishes with little or no oil. While I love enjoying a table-top donabe-steamed dish, I also often keep it on the stove for prepping vegetables. Instead of blanching in hot water, I prefer steaming vegetables, as it enhances flavour, improves texture and helps retain more nutrients. If you remove the steam grate, a donabe steamer can also function as a classic-style donabe.

TAGINE-STYLE DONABE: While a traditional donabe is commonly used for soupy or stewed dishes, this style is a *toban* – an earthenware frying pan (skillet) – featuring a tall, dome-shaped lid inspired by the Moroccan tagine. In recent years, tagine-style donabe have gained popularity in Japan for their versatility, serving as a crossover between a pot and a sauté pan. You can use it as a shallow pot for quick-simmered dishes or for stir-frying and pan-frying ingredients. The tall lid creates extra space, allowing for enhanced steaming effects while cooking, helping to retain moisture and bring out deeper flavours.

CHOOSING BY SIZE AND SHAPE

Size is another important factor when selecting a donabe, especially if you plan to own just one. Choosing the right size ensures that it fits your cooking needs and serves the right number of people. There are no standardised size indicators – one product's 'large' may be 1.8 litres (60 fl oz), while another could be 3 litres (100 fl oz). The classification is often relative, so I recommend checking the actual capacity rather than relying on size labels when purchasing.

For a classic-style donabe, a size up to 1 litre (34 fl oz) is ideal for a single serving of hotpot or a one-pot noodle dish. When used for rice, soup or an appetiser as part of a meal, it can comfortably serve two people. A donabe up to 1.8 litres (60 fl oz) is good for two to three people, while one up to 2.5 litres (85 fl oz) works well for up to five people. Of course, it depends on the kind of dish you're making and how you plan to serve it.

If you're getting just one donabe to begin with, I usually recommend choosing a slightly larger size, as it can handle smaller portions with no problem and you can also fill it to capacity when cooking for more, especially when you're entertaining. That flexibility makes it especially practical for everyday use.

In addition to size, the shape of a donabe also affects its functionality. A wider donabe is ideal if you want to spread large or multiple ingredients in a single layer. A deeper donabe is often better suited to soups and stews.

CHOOSING BY OTHER FACTORS

DRY-HEATING CAPABILITY: Traditional donabe cannot be heated without liquid inside, as the clay may crack under direct high heat. However, dry-heating-capable donabe are made with highly durable clay and glaze, allowing you to heat an empty donabe or cook ingredients without any liquid. This type of donabe is ideal if you want to dry-roast, stir-fry or sear ingredients over higher heat. When purchasing a donabe, check the product details or ask the maker to confirm whether it is dry-heating capable.

INDUCTION OR ELECTRIC STOVETOP COMPATIBILITY: For centuries, donabe have been used over direct flame – originally over wood fires; in more recent years, on gas stoves. Because a donabe is made of earthenware, it is naturally not compatible with induction or electric stovetops. However, as more households are now equipped with electric or induction heating (IH), a growing number of donabe are being made with a magnetic plate attached to the bottom, allowing them to work with these heat sources. When purchasing a donabe, check the product details or look for an indication that it is IH- or electric-compatible.

AESTHETIC DESIGN: If you have done some research but still can't decide which donabe to choose, following your aesthetic taste is a great approach. Different artisans bring their own styles to donabe – from classic to unique colours, cute shaped handles to no handles, and smooth, glossy finishes to rustic, coarse textures. The variations are endless, making the selection process both fun and personal. I always feel that the look of a donabe brings joy to the home, so instead of hiding them in a cupboard, I display my donabe collection on shelves as part of my kitchen's décor.

How to Care for Your Donabe

A donabe is designed for everyday use. Once you understand the basics of caring for it, it's easy to maintain. No special care is needed, just simple steps to keep it in great condition. Here is what to do when you get a new donabe and how to properly care for it to ensure it lasts for years to come.

MEDOME (DONABE SEASONING)

The very first and most important step after getting a new donabe is seasoning it, a process known as *medome* in Japanese. Some people worry that seasoning might be difficult or that they could break their donabe, but there is no need to worry! Medome is a simple, one-time process that strengthens the donabe's naturally porous clay body. It's also a special moment – your first interaction with your new donabe. To me, seasoning a donabe is always a therapeutic experience. The process is easy: cook a thick porridge in the donabe using pre-cooked rice and water. The starch from the rice fills tiny gaps in the clay, reinforcing its durability and helping to prevent cracks or leaks. It also helps to create a natural barrier, making the donabe less likely to absorb strong food aromas from future cooking.

STEP-BY-STEP MEDOME

Before starting the medome process, rinse the inside of your donabe with clean water. Make sure the bottom of the donabe is completely dry before placing it on the stove. Some donabe, including toban, may not require medome. Check the product details before seasoning your donabe.

1. **ADD COOKED RICE AND WATER:** Add cooked rice (leftover rice works well) to the donabe, to about a quarter to a fifth of its capacity. Add water until the donabe is about 80 per cent full. No precise measurements are needed – just eyeball it.

2. **COOK OVER LOW HEAT:** Place the donabe on the stove and start with low heat. Slowly bring the mixture to a gentle simmer to allow the clay to warm up gradually. No lid is needed.

3. **SIMMER ON LOW HEAT:** Once the porridge starts to simmer, keep it on low heat until it becomes very thick. This could take about 30 minutes or longer for a medium-size donabe. Stir occasionally to prevent sticking.

4. **LET IT COOL:** Turn off the heat and let the donabe cool down naturally for at least 1 hour or longer.

5. **DISCARD AND RINSE:** Discard the porridge and rinse the donabe with clean water – no soap needed.

6. **AIR-DRY COMPLETELY:** Let the donabe air-dry completely before storing or using it for cooking. If you plan to use it immediately after seasoning, rinse only the inside and make sure the bottom is completely dry before placing it over the heat.

Donabe Care Do's and Don'ts

DO →

KEEP THE BOTTOM DRY BEFORE HEATING: Before placing a donabe on the stove, make sure the bottom is completely dry. If moisture is trapped in the porous clay, it can expand with heat and lead to cracks.

DO →

LET YOUR DONABE DRY COMPLETELY BEFORE STORING: After rinsing your donabe, turn it upside down to air-dry thoroughly. Leaving it overnight is ideal. Storing a damp donabe can lead to mould, especially in humid environments.

DO →

EMBRACE THE NATURAL AGEING OF YOUR DONABE: Over time, the interior of your donabe will develop *kannyu* – tiny crackles in the glaze caused by natural expansion and contraction during cooking. This is completely normal and enhances the donabe's character. The kannyu may darken or spread with use, creating a beautiful patina. Your donabe may also develop small chips on the edges over time. As long as they don't affect its function, they are nothing to worry about. These natural changes reflect the donabe's journey and are part of its wabisabi beauty – the Japanese appreciation of imperfection and time-worn elegance. As you continue cooking with your donabe, it becomes even more personal, carrying the warmth and memories of every meal.

DON'T →

EXPOSE DONABE TO SUDDEN TEMPERATURE CHANGES: Avoid thermal shock, as abrupt temperature changes can cause cracking. Never place a cold donabe directly over high heat or pour cold water into a hot donabe. If you are unsure of your donabe's durability and a recipe calls for high heat, start with low to moderate heat for a few minutes before increasing to high.

DON'T →

HEAT DONABE WITHOUT LIQUID OR USE FOR FRYING: A traditional donabe is not designed to be heated without liquid, as this can cause cracking. It is also not suitable for deep-frying or pan-frying. The porous clay cannot withstand prolonged direct contact with oil at high temperatures, which may damage the donabe and pose a fire risk. If your donabe is dry-heating capable, you can safely heat it without liquid for dry-roasting or pan-frying. Otherwise, if you need to fry or pan-fry ingredients, use a separate pan and transfer them to the donabe afterwards. That said, most traditional donabe can be used for sautéing with a small amount of oil over moderate heat without issue.

About This Book

You are what you eat. The way you choose ingredients and plan your meals can nourish not just your body, but also your soul. Cooking with intention – whether it's a simple meal for yourself or a beautifully prepared donabe feast for guests – brings another level of fulfilment. Taking the time to appreciate the process and the presentation makes every dish more meaningful. So, I hope this book inspires you to slow down, savour the moment and find satisfaction in the simple joy of cooking. That's the spirit of a happy donabe life.

MY COOKING STYLE

This book is filled with my personal recipes, rooted in Japanese home cooking – dishes I love and make often. My cooking style blends traditional and modern Japanese techniques with international influences, including Mediterranean flavours (I love extra virgin olive oil!). It reflects my life journey – learning from my mother and grandmother, growing up in cosmopolitan Tokyo, travelling the world and living in Los Angeles for many years. I am constantly curious and inspired by the ingredients, flavours and cultures I encounter, and my cooking naturally evolves with them. Donabe cooking often involves simmering, stewing, steaming and other gentle one-pot methods, bringing out the best flavours of the ingredients and making it easy to create well-balanced meals. While I am not vegetarian or vegan, my cooking is vegetable-forward, and donabe cooking helps me enjoy more vegetables in my daily meals. I naturally keep a *yakuzen* mindset (page 22), based on the traditional Eastern philosophy of food as medicine, which values balance and the natural benefits of ingredients. Simple Japanese home cooking and a donabe-centred approach to meals have kept me healthy for decades (and my weight hasn't changed since I was 12!). There are no deep-fried recipes in this book, but I'm confident you won't miss them!

HOW TO STRUCTURE A DONABE MEAL

The recipes in this book are divided into the following categories: Small Bites (appetisers and side dishes); Vegetarian Mains; Seafood Mains; Meat Mains; Rice, Noodles and Grains; Wagashi Sweets; and Dashi, Sauces and Condiments.

When I cook a multi-course meal, I usually serve 2–3 appetisers, followed by a main donabe dish, then a rice or noodle donabe dish, and finally dessert. A more casual home dinner might include 1–2 side dishes, a main donabe dish and donabe rice, all served together. But there are no rules – sometimes a meal can be as simple as a selection of small appetisers and sides, or just one side dish paired with a donabe rice or noodle dish.

Dishes categorised as mains can also be served as appetisers, depending on portion size and presentation. The possibilities are endless, and I hope this book inspires you to mix and match dishes in ways that suit your meals best.

THE ART OF SHIME: THE FINISHING COURSE

In donabe cooking, *shime* (pronounced 'shee-may') refers to the satisfying final course made by simmering noodles, rice or grains in the remaining broth of a hotpot meal. After everyone has enjoyed the main ingredients, the broth becomes especially precious, infused with all the umami from the meat, vegetables and seasonings. Many people look forward to shime and even save room just for it.

It's also a naturally balanced way to enjoy carbs. In a traditional Japanese course-based meal, rice or noodles are typically served at the end rather than the beginning. Eating carbs later in the meal can help prevent blood sugar spikes – just one more reason to slow down and enjoy this comforting final course.

Here's a simple guide to creating your own delicious shime at home:

1. RESERVE THE BROTH: You can't make shime without broth. If you plan to enjoy a finishing course, be sure to save enough broth before the pot is emptied. You can also prepare a little extra broth ahead of time to top off the donabe before starting the shime and adjust the seasoning if needed.

2. WHAT TO ADD: There are no set rules, just follow your appetite and imagination. Popular choices include par-cooked udon or ramen, cooked rice, soba, mochi or even dried pasta. Depending on the broth and your mood, you can keep it simple or add ingredients like a beaten egg, a sprinkle of cheese, a pat of butter or fresh herbs. You can even use leftover broth the next day to make a quick takikomi gohan (mixed rice) – no longer a finishing course, but still incredibly satisfying.

3. HOW MUCH BROTH IS NEEDED: The amount of broth depends on the type and quantity of starch you're adding. Always bring the broth to a high simmer before adding the starch.

→ For par-cooked noodles or cooked rice, aim for enough broth to just cover the ingredients – a 1:2 to 2:3 ratio of starch to broth (by volume) is a good guideline.

→ If using dried noodles, add about 150–200 ml (5–7 fl oz/scant ⅔–scant 1 cup) extra water per serving to the broth before cooking, since they absorb more liquid.

4. HOW LONG TO COOK:

→ Par-cooked noodles like udon or soba need just 1–2 minutes.

→ For ojiya (soupy rice porridge), simmer cooked rice for 2–3 minutes or until it turns to smooth porridge consistency, then add beaten egg and let it gently set.

→ For dried noodles or pasta, follow the package instructions and adjust depending on the broth's thickness.

Shime is not just a way to finish a hotpot meal, it's the essence of a happy donabe life.

If a dish is good for shime, you'll find a note in the applicable hotpot-style recipes in the main dish chapters.

YAKUZEN: FOOD IS MEDICINE

Yakuzen (薬膳) is a traditional Eastern approach to therapeutic food, rooted in Chinese medicine with over 2,000 years of history. Over time, it's been adapted into Japanese home cooking to support overall wellness and help prevent illness. Rather than treating symptoms in isolation, yakuzen encourages tuning into your body's signals and nourishing it in ways that promote long-term balance.

Meals inspired by yakuzen follow seasonal rhythms and ingredient properties, supporting key functions like digestion, circulation and energy. The core theory revolves around balancing 気 (*ki* or *qi* – vital energy), 血 (*ketsu* – blood) and 水 (*sui* – fluids), which sustain both physical and emotional well-being.

You don't have to be an expert to benefit from the ideas of yakuzen. With a little curiosity and a mindful approach to cooking, anyone can enjoy its everyday wisdom. For me, it's often as simple as reaching for cooling vegetables in summer, warming root vegetables in winter, or making porridge when my stomach feels off. They've become part of my everyday rhythm in the kitchen.

Throughout the book, I point out ingredients or combinations that may support your well-being. This isn't a yakuzen cookbook, but I hope these small insights inspire you to tune into your body, eat mindfully and enjoy the comforting rhythm of cooking with care.

CHOOSING HIGH-QUALITY INGREDIENTS

Quality matters the most. It can be an investment sometimes, but sourcing high-quality, natural ingredients with no or minimal additives, as much as possible, is essential for bringing out the best flavours in a dish. Staples such as shoyu and miso are especially important – you want to choose ingredients you will enjoy eating on their own. My mom used to say, 'If you have a bottle of high-quality artisan shoyu, you don't really need anything else.' Great ingredients do most of the work for you, allowing flavours to shine with simple preparation. For produce, seasonality plays a big role in quality, so choose seasonal ingredients whenever possible.

ADAPTING RECIPES AND SUBSTITUTIONS

My recipes are meant to inspire you – they serve as guidelines, not strict rules. Feel free to adjust them to your taste, ingredients on hand or the appliances you use. Heat levels can vary depending on your stove or cookware, so you may need to modify the heat or cooking time accordingly. Many ingredients in this book are easy to substitute or even omit based on availability or preference, and even recipes using animal protein can often be adapted with plant-based alternatives. Especially with condiments and toppings, I encourage you to switch things around to suit your mood or what you already have. I have included suggestions in the recipe notes, but you can always experiment to find what works best for you. Most importantly, trust your own judgement and have fun in the kitchen!

DONABE AND ALTERNATIVE COOKWARE

Many recipes in this book are designed for donabe cooking, but they can be adapted using other cookware. While I hope you'll experience the joy of cooking with donabe, I understand not everyone has one on hand. Here are the types of donabe used in this book, with suggested alternatives. Each recipe notes the donabe type (and size, for classic-style). If using other cookware, keep in mind that cooking times and heat adjustments may vary depending on the material and heat retention.

CLASSIC-STYLE DONABE, INCLUDING DONABE FOR SOUPS, STEWS AND BRAISING: These are the most versatile styles and can be used interchangeably for many recipes. The donabe rice cooker and donabe steamer can also double as classic-style donabe when needed. I use different sizes throughout the book, but that doesn't mean you need every size. A recipe for a 1.2 litre (40 fl oz) donabe can be cooked in a 1.8 litre (60 fl oz) donabe. If using a smaller one, reduce the recipe amounts accordingly.
Alternative cookware: casserole dish (Dutch oven), enamelled cast-iron pot, or heavy-based stainless-steel pot with a lid.

DONABE RICE COOKER: I use a 3 rice-cup size (1.5 litre/50 fl oz) double-lid rice cooker made by Nagatani-en. It cooks rice quickly and evenly without needing to adjust the heat. Any donabe with enough depth can be used, although the method may vary. When this donabe is used in recipes, I also include a basic stovetop method.
Alternative cookware: casserole dish (Dutch oven), enamelled cast-iron pot, or a heavy-based stainless-steel pot with a lid.

DONABE STEAMER: Designed with a removable steam grate, this donabe is used for all steaming recipes in the book. I use a 3 litre (100 fl oz) donabe steamer.
Alternative cookware: A pot with a steam basket or a multi-tiered steamer.

TAGINE-STYLE DONABE: This toban-style donabe has a tall lid and is ideal for sizzling, pan-frying, stir-frying or quick simmering with minimal liquid. Most recipes using this donabe can be adapted to a classic-style donabe with a wide base. For dry-heat or high-heat methods, be sure your donabe is safe for those uses.
Alternative cookware: Cast-iron frying pan (skillet) (30 cm/12 in diameter or 500 ml/17 fl oz capacity), heavy-based sauté pan with a lid.

Measurements & Guides

MEASUREMENTS

This book follows the metric system. Some measurements are approximate.

1 TEASPOON = 5 ML

1 TABLESPOON = 15 ML

100 G = 3½ OZ

100 ML = 3½ FL OZ

240 ML = 1 US CUP

1 LITRE = 1 QUART

1 RICE CUP* = 180 ML
(6 FL OZ/¾ CUP)/150 G (5½ OZ)

NOTE: A rice cup, or '*go*' (合), is a traditional Japanese measurement commonly used for rice.

DIETARY GUIDE

Many recipes in this book are naturally vegan or vegetarian, and even those that include animal protein can often be easily adapted. To help you find recipes that fit your preferences, where applicable, you will find the following labels on recipe pages:

- VG — **VEGAN:** Plant-based. Contains no animal products.
- VG OP — **VEGAN OPTION:** A non-vegan recipe with easy modifications to make it vegan.
- VE — **VEGETARIAN:** Contains no meat or seafood but may include dairy or eggs.
- VE OP — **VEGETARIAN OPTION:** A non-vegetarian recipe with easy modifications to make it vegetarian.
- GF — **GLUTEN-FREE:** Contains no wheat gluten.
- GF OP — **GLUTEN-FREE OPTION:** A non-gluten-free recipe with easy modifications to make it gluten-free.

西京
白みそ
匠
Gluten Free No MSG added
八丁味噌
Hatcho Miso
賞味期限:
26. 5. 20
Ohsawa
Brown Rice Miso
Organic & Unpasteurized
NET 9 OZ. (255 g)
Ohsawa
国産有機醤油
PRODUCT OF JAPAN
Artisan Amber
Rice Vinegar
純米
富士酢
PREMIUM
GEKKEIKAN
月桂冠
胡麻油

My Absolute Essentials

Here are the key Japanese seasonings I always keep in my refrigerator or pantry. They are the foundation for building flavour in everyday cooking.

MISO

There are so many kinds of miso – different styles, colours and brands – and the salt content can vary widely. I usually keep several in my refrigerator: my homemade miso, three or four kinds of kome miso, Saikyo miso and Hatcho miso. I enjoy switching between different types rather than sticking to just one, and I often blend two for soups to add depth and variety. I sometimes use mugi or chickpea miso too, depending on how I feel. You don't need to stock as many as I do, but I encourage you to try a few, taste them on their own, and enjoy matching different misos to different dishes.
Here are the kinds I use in this book:

KOME MISO (made from soybeans and rice koji): This is the most common type of miso, and what I mean when I list just 'miso' in this book. They can be aged about 9 months to a few years. Salt content can vary between 10 per cent and up to 15 per cent, so adjust the amount you use accordingly. The miso used in my recipes are about 12 per cent salt content. The colour can range from pale white to beige to dark red. Use a kind you like the taste of on its own.

SAIKYO MISO or SWEET WHITE MISO (also made from soybeans and rice koji): While it's technically a type of kome miso, I treat it as its own category. Saikyo miso is a Kyoto-style sweet white miso, made with extra rice koji – about twice as much rice to soybeans – and only about 5 per cent salt. It's also aged for just 2–4 weeks, so the flavour is delicate and naturally sweet.

HATCHO MISO (made from soybeans and koji): This miso has a deep flavour and dark colour. Koji mould is inoculated directly on the soybeans instead of rice, and the aging period can be 1–3 years. The salt content is usually around 10–12 per cent, but the flavour is so concentrated that a little goes a long way. Hatcho miso is made only in Aichi Prefecture. Similar miso made in other regions is called mame miso ('bean' miso).

Once purchased, miso should be kept refrigerated. Once you open a package, regardless of the 'best before' date, I suggest using the miso within a few months to best enjoy its fresh, 'live' flavour. If kept too long, the flavour can start to taste tired.

SHOYU (SOY SAUCE)

There are different types of soy sauce in Japanese cooking, and I use a few kinds depending on the dish. Unless otherwise noted, when I say 'shoyu' in this book, I'm referring to regular all-purpose koikuchi shoyu, which is the most common type in Japan. I also use tamari, usukuchi shoyu and sometimes shiro shoyu depending on the flavour or colour I want in the dish. When choosing shoyu, I recommend looking for traditionally brewed kinds with no additives – just water, soybeans, wheat, salt and koji. They have a much rounder, cleaner flavour and make a big difference in cooking.

KOIKUCHI SHOYU (made from water, soybeans, wheat, salt and fermented with koji): This is the standard Japanese soy sauce found in most home kitchens and restaurants. I refer to it simply as 'shoyu' in the recipes throughout this book. While it contains a small amount of wheat, the gluten is mostly broken down during fermentation, so the final product has only minimal traces.

TAMARI SHOYU OR TAMARI (soy sauce made without wheat): Commonly referred to simply as tamari, this type of soy sauce is brewed without wheat and is naturally gluten-free. It has a darker colour, slightly thicker consistency and a more concentrated flavour than regular shoyu. I often use it when I want a bolder taste, richer colour or extra shine in a dish. It also works well as a gluten-free substitute for regular shoyu.

USUKUCHI SHOYU (light-coloured soy sauce): Often called just usukuchi, this light-coloured soy sauce has a higher salt content than regular shoyu, despite its pale appearance. I use it when I want to season without darkening the colour of the dish, especially in clear broths or gently simmered dishes. I sometimes blend it with regular shoyu to add depth and balance.

SHIRO SHOYU (white soy sauce): This type of soy sauce is made mostly from wheat with just a small amount of soybeans. It has a pale amber colour and lighter flavour with less umami than regular shoyu. I use it when I want to season gently and let the ingredients' natural colours and flavours shine. There is also a kind made from 100 per cent wheat flour with no soybeans, called shiro tamari (white tamari), which has an extra-mellow flavour. Either one works when shiro shoyu is called for in a recipe.

Once opened, I suggest storing shoyu in the refrigerator to help maintain its aroma and flavour. Over time, the taste can fade, so I try to use it within a few months for best results.

SAKE

I use **JUNMAI SAKE** in my cooking, which is made purely from rice, water and koji. It's used to bring subtle complexity, balance and a gentle roundness to a dish. It can also help ingredients absorb seasoning more evenly and give a nice shine to simmered dishes. Good Honjozo sake, made from rice, water, koji and some added alcohol, can also work with cooking. There's no need to use expensive sake like daiginjo – an affordable junmai works well. I avoid 'cooking sake', since it often contains added salt and other additives.

Once opened, I keep sake in the refrigerator and try to use it within a few weeks. If you're not using sake, depending on the dish, you can often substitute with dashi or water.

MIRIN

I use **HON MIRIN** (genuine mirin), which is traditionally brewed from glutinous rice (sweet rice), rice koji and shochu. Its natural sweetness comes from slow fermentation, not from added sugars or sweeteners, and the alcohol content is typically around 13–14 per cent. It's the kind of mirin you can even sip on its own. Hon mirin adds depth, gloss and gentle umami to simmered dishes and sauces, and helps bring all the flavours together.

Some products labelled as hon mirin are made through faster, industrial methods and may include sweeteners like corn syrup. There are also mirin-style seasonings that contain additives and artificial flavours. I recommend checking the label and choosing real hon mirin – one made purely through fermentation, with no added sugar or synthetic ingredients.

Once opened, I store it in a cool, dark place or in the refrigerator and try to use it within a few months to enjoy its best flavour. If needed, mirin can be substituted with raw brown sugar or maple syrup, although the depth and umami won't be the same. If substituting, use about two-thirds of the amount called for in the recipe.

RICE VINEGAR

Made from fermented rice, Japanese rice vinegar has a mild, slightly sweet acidity that adds balance without being sharp. I use it in dressings, marinades, pickles and sushi rice. Compared to Western-style vinegar, the acidity is much milder (usually around 4 per cent), so it blends easily with other seasonings. Once opened, I store it in a cool, dark place or in the refrigerator.

KUROZU (JAPANESE BLACK VINEGAR)

KUROZU is a traditional Japanese black vinegar made from brown rice through long, slow fermentation. It has a deep, mellow acidity with natural sweetness and umami. I use it in dipping sauces and dressings, or splash it over simmered dishes when I want gentle acidity with more body than regular rice vinegar. It's quite different from Chinese black vinegar, which is often made from a mix of rice, wheat, barley or sorghum, and tends to have a sharper, more robust flavour. Once opened, I store it in a cool, dark place or in the refrigerator.

SALT

I use natural sea salt in this book, most often moshio – a traditional Japanese sea salt made with seaweed. It has a mild, rounded flavour that adds subtle umami. You don't need to use the same kind; any high-quality sea salt will work. Depending on the type – whether it's finer or flakier – you may want to adjust the amount slightly, since finer salt tends to pack more densely and taste saltier by volume.

SUGAR

I mainly use sugar to add balance and flavour complexity to savoury dishes, not to make them taste sweet. I often use raw brown sugar for its mild, rounded flavour. I also like Okinawa black sugar, which is an unrefined cane sugar made by slowly cooking down sugarcane juice. It's considered a type of brown sugar, but its colour is much darker and the flavour is deeper, with a complex mineral-rich sweetness. For desserts, instead of sugar, I often substitute with erythritol or monk fruit sweetener, especially the kind blended with allulose (a natural, plant-derived sweetener that lets me enjoy a zero-sugar dessert without compromising flavour or quality).

OIL

Oil isn't used in large amounts in traditional Japanese cooking, but a small splash can bring balance or a nice finish to a dish. I keep a few types in my pantry: light- and dark-roasted sesame oil, plus extra virgin olive oil. Depending on how much aroma I want, I switch between light and dark sesame oil – each brings a different character to the dish. Extra virgin olive oil isn't traditional, but I find it works surprisingly well with Japanese flavours, and I use it often for both cooking and finishing. Occasionally, I also use coconut oil, avocado oil or algae oil. Algae oil has a very neutral taste and is great for high-heat cooking. I usually avoid other types of vegetable oils, and stick with oils that feel better for both flavour and how I want to eat. Oils can oxidise more quickly once opened, so I store them in a cool, dark place and try to use them within 1–2 months to maintain their aroma and quality.

Butter is also something I love – who doesn't love butter? I often use it in savoury dishes to add finishing aroma and depth. It pairs especially well with shoyu. For a plant-based option, you can substitute butter with extra virgin olive oil or coconut oil (if you prefer a solid oil).

6/2
Shio-Koji

MY SHOP, TOIRO

Where a Happy Donabe Life Begins

TOIRO is the expression of my lifestyle, and I created it to share the joy of donabe cooking and a healthy Japanese way of living. At the shop, you'll find a wide array of artisan Iga-yaki donabe, kitchen tools, tableware and pantry items – everything you need for donabe cooking and for the recipes in this book, carefully sourced from Japan and beyond. Every piece is something I personally love and has a story behind it.

Today, we're lucky to welcome customers from all over the world, and it brings me so much happiness to share the joy and beautiful rituals of donabe life – little moments that I believe can bring more *ikigai* (life purpose) to everyday living.

Our brick-and-mortar shop is in West Hollywood, and our online store ships across the US and internationally (excluding food and some restricted items).

TOIRO

1257 N. LA BREA AVENUE,
WEST HOLLYWOOD, CA 90038, USA

TOIROKITCHEN.COM

II

SMALL BITES

My meals always begin with small bites, often simple ae-mono – lightly dressed or mixed vegetable dishes. These comforting dishes set the tone for the meal, serving as appetisers or side dishes. Sometimes, I like to combine a few small dishes to make a meal on their own, or to pack for obento (lunchboxes) or a picnic. They're incredibly flexible and can be enjoyed in different ways. The recipes in this chapter are naturally plant-based, with many reflecting the deep influence of shojin ryori (Buddhist temple cuisine) on Japanese home cooking. Most of them can be prepared in advance, making them both convenient and versatile.

Yamagata Dashi

YAMAGATA-STYLE CHILLED CHOPPED VEGETABLE SAUCE

山形だし

Serves 4

5 okra
1 Japanese aubergine (eggplant) (about 100 g/3½ oz), peeled in alternating stripes and diced into 5 mm (¼ in) cubes
1 small cucumber (ideally Japanese cucumber) (about 100 g/3½ oz), peeled in alternating stripes and diced into 5 mm (¼ in) cubes
100 g (3½ oz) nagaimo (Japanese mountain yam), peeled and diced into 5 mm (¼ in) cubes
5 g (¼ oz) dried mekabu seaweed or mixed seaweed, rehydrated and chopped, if needed
80 g (2¾ oz) shelled, cooked edamame
15 g (½ oz) fresh root ginger, very finely julienned
3-4 tbsp Kaeshi (page 239)
2 tbsp water, or as needed
2-3 shiso leaves, finely julienned
sea salt, to taste

A beloved summer staple from Yamagata, a northern region of Japan, Yamagata dashi is a finely chopped vegetable dish typically enjoyed on its own or over tofu, rice or noodles. I also love it over grilled fish or meat. Despite its name – dashi – this is not a soup stock. It's a refreshing mix of sliced okra, diced raw aubergine (eggplant), cucumber and other seasonal vegetables, lightly seasoned with my homemade multi-purpose soy-based umami sauce, Kaeshi (page 239). Since this dish is all about flexibility, there's no need to measure precisely – adjust, substitute or omit ingredients based on what you have on hand.

METHOD: Bring a saucepan of water to the boil, add the okra and blanch for 30 seconds. Drain and rinse with cold water. Cut into thin slices widthways.

Place the aubergine and cucumber in a bowl of lightly salted water and soak for 5–10 minutes. Drain and rinse with cold water. Drain well again.

Combine the okra, aubergine, cucumber, nagaimo, seaweed, edamame and ginger in a bowl. Add the kaeshi and water, then mix well with a spoon until smooth and slightly sticky in texture. Adjust the amount of water, if needed. Cover and refrigerate for at least 1 hour or overnight to let the flavours meld.

Mix in the shiso and serve cool or chilled.

Sayaingen Kurumi Miso-Ae

GREEN BEANS IN WALNUT MISO CREAM

さやいんげんの
胡桃味噌和え

Serves 4

300 g (10½ oz) green beans, stem ends trimmed
1 recipe quantity Kurumi Miso (page 241)

Green beans are incredibly versatile and perfect for make-ahead dishes. While you can simply blanch them, I prefer steaming, as it enhances their flavour and helps retain more nutrients. I like to cook them until just tender with a slight crunch for the best texture. The bright flavours of the green beans pair really well with the creamy and nutty kurumi miso – I often find myself eating a large bowl of it on my own!

This dish may help ease puffiness and gently restores energy. It is thought that green beans support fluid balance, while walnuts warm and nourish the body and brain. Together, they help relieve fatigue and will revitalise you.

EQUIPMENT: Donabe steamer (or pot with a steam basket)

METHOD: Set up the donabe steamer and bring the water to the boil. Arrange the green beans on the grate, cover and steam over a medium-high heat for 2–3 minutes, or until just tender.

Let the beans cool slightly, then cut them in half at an angle. Toss with the kurumi miso in a bowl and transfer to a serving plate. Serve cool or at room temperature.

NOTE: This dish is also great for obento (lunchboxes) or a picnic.

Hakko Otsumami Trio

PROBIOTIC SMALL BITES WITH FERMENTED FLAVOURS

発酵おつまみ三種

Serves 4–6

For the miso-marinated tofu

- 1 x 400 g (14oz) package medium-firm tofu, cut in half
- 120 g (4 oz/½ cup) miso
- 1½–2 tbsp maple syrup

For the yuzu miso dipping sauce

- 4 tbsp miso
- 2 tbsp yuzu marmalade (or orange marmalade)

For the sake-kasu shio-koji dipping sauce

- 4 tbsp sake-kasu (see Note)
- 1½ tbsp Shio-Koji (page 238)
- ½ tbsp toasted sesame oil
- 1 tbsp toasted white sesame seeds

To serve

- shiso leaves
- wasabi
- crackers, vegetable crudités, fruit and nuts, as desired

These marinated tofu and dips are simple to prepare yet packed with rich flavours and health benefits, thanks to the fermented ingredients miso, sake-kasu and shio-koji. They are prepared without heating, preserving the probiotics and enzymes from the fermentation process. The miso-marinated tofu becomes creamier and denser after a couple of days of marinating, with a delicate miso flavour that's truly delightful. The two dipping sauces come together in minutes, perfect for last-minute guests. They pair especially well with crisp vegetables or can be topped with nuts for added texture.

METHOD: For the miso-marinated tofu, place the tofu in a shallow tray and top with a flat tray or small cutting board. Add a weight 1–1.5 times the tofu's weight and let it sit for 30 minutes to remove excess moisture. Drain the liquid and pat the tofu dry with a paper towel.

To prepare the marinade, whisk together the miso and maple syrup in a bowl until smooth.

Wrap each tofu piece in a small piece of muslin (cheesecloth). On a sheet of cling film (plastic wrap), spread a quarter of the miso marinade. Place a tofu piece on top, then spread another quarter of the marinade evenly over it. Wrap tightly in the cling film, gently pressing to ensure the tofu is fully coated in marinade. Repeat with the second piece of tofu. Marinate in the refrigerator for 2 days, or up to 5 days for deeper flavour.

For the dipping sauces, whisk together their respective ingredients in separate bowls until smooth. Transfer to individual serving bowls. They can both be made a day in advance and stored in the refrigerator.

Gently unwrap the tofu and slice as desired. Serve on shiso leaves, topping each piece with a dab of wasabi. Arrange with the dipping sauces, crackers, vegetable crudités, fruits and nuts on a serving board for a beautiful and inviting spread.

NOTE: Sake-kasu (sake lees) is the nutrient-rich by-product of sake brewing, packed with amino acids and enzymes. I love using the soft paste, but if using the block form, warm it slightly and mix in a bit of sake or water to soften. It does contain trace amounts of alcohol. Sake-kasu is great for marinades, pickles, soups, dressings and even desserts. Store it in an airtight container in the refrigerator or freeze it for longer storage.

FLAVOUR VARIATION: For the sake-kasu dip, the sesame seeds can be substituted with freshly grated Parmesan for a non-vegan option. Reduce the shio-koji by about ½ tablespoon to adjust the saltiness. It's umami rich and so good, too!

Aka Cabbage Shio-Kombu Salad

RED CABBAGE AND SHIO-KOMBU SALAD

赤キャベツと
塩昆布のサラダ

Serves 4

- 200 g (7 oz) red cabbage, finely shredded
- 1 heaped tsp sea salt
- 50 g (1¾ oz) walnuts
- 2 tbsp shio-kombu (seasoned shredded kelp; see Note)
- 2–3 tbsp chopped mint leaves or your choice of herbs (optional)
- 1 tbsp extra virgin olive oil, or more to taste

This is one of my go-to salads – simple, flavourful and a great complement to almost any meal. Lightly salt-marinating the cabbage draws out excess moisture, leaving it tender yet still crisp. Shio-kombu, or seasoned kelp, is an umami-rich condiment made from shredded kombu simmered with shoyu and other seasonings. It enhances the natural sweetness of the cabbage and adds depth. In Japan, it's a staple often sprinkled over rice or salads, and it works beautifully in this dish.

I like to mix in fresh herbs like mint – or whatever I have on hand – for an extra refreshing touch. The measurements below are quite loose. I usually just eyeball everything when I make this, so I hope you can do the same!

METHOD: Mix the red cabbage with the salt in a bowl and let it rest for 30 minutes. After this time, transfer the cabbage to a clean tea towel (dish cloth) and squeeze out the excess moisture.

Meanwhile, preheat the oven to 180°C/350°F (160°C/320°F fan). Spread the walnuts over a baking sheet and roast for 7–8 minutes, or until lightly golden and fragrant. Let them cool, then coarsely chop or break by hand.

Combine the cabbage, walnuts, shio-kombu, mint (if using) and olive oil in a mixing bowl. Toss well to mix, then transfer to a serving bowl. Serve cool or chilled.

NOTE: Shio-kombu's salt level varies by brand, so taste and adjust as needed. I prefer brands with no or minimum additives.

FLAVOUR VARIATION: For a non-vegetarian twist, replace the shio-kombu with jako (dried baby sardines).

Murasaki-Imo Goma Almond Butter Sauce-Ae

ROASTED PURPLE SWEET POTATO IN SESAME ALMOND BUTTER SAUCE

紫芋の胡麻アーモンドバターソース和え

Serves 4

- 1 medium-large purple sweet potato (about 500 g/1 lb 2 oz)
- 1 quantity Goma Almond Butter Sauce (page 242)
- 1 tbsp extra virgin olive oil
- 150 g (5½ oz) Tenderstem broccoli (broccolini), cut into 3 cm (1 in) pieces
- 2 tbsp water
- sea salt and freshly ground black pepper
- roasted sliced almonds, to garnish

I love the vibrant colour, texture and flavour of this combination. The natural sweetness of purple sweet potato pairs beautifully with the nutty richness of sesame and almond butter. As the sweet potato mixes with the sauce, it naturally breaks apart, creating a lightly mashed texture that still retains some bite. The sweet potato is delicious on its own, but the addition of sautéed Tenderstem broccoli (broccolini) adds a touch of bitterness and a crisp-tender bite. Together, they make a balanced and deeply satisfying dish.

METHOD: Preheat the oven to 200°C/400°F (180°C/350°F fan). Roast the sweet potato for 30–45 minutes, or until a skewer easily pierces through. Let it cool down slightly for easier handling, then peel the skin by trimming the ends with a small knife – the skin should come off easily by hand.

Slice the sweet potato into large bite-size pieces (they don't have to be even) and transfer to a bowl. Add the goma almond butter sauce and gently mix with a spatula. It's fine if the sauce isn't evenly mixed – this variation in texture and flavour makes each bite more interesting.

Heat the olive oil in a sauté pan over a medium heat. Add the broccoli and cook for 1–2 minutes, then add the water, cover and steam for 2–3 minutes until the water has evaporated and the broccoli is tender. Season with salt and pepper.

Scoop the sweet potato mixture onto a serving plate or bowl. Arrange the broccoli on top or alongside and garnish with roasted sliced almonds. Serve warm or at room temperature.

NOTE: This dish is also great for obento (lunchboxes) or a picnic.

FLAVOUR VARIATION: You can swap the broccoli for any other vegetables of your choice. Grilled asparagus is also great.

Corn Tofu

CORN KUDZU JELLY CAKE
とうもろこしの葛豆腐

Serves 4–6

2 corn-on-the-cobs
(about 250 g/8 oz kernels)
360 ml (12 fl oz/1.5 cups)
water
4 tsp sea salt, or more
to taste
45 g (1.5 oz) kudzu starch
(see Note)
1 okra, blanched and
thinly sliced widthways,
to garnish (optional)
wasabi paste, to serve

If you are a fan of traditional Japanese cuisine, especially *shojin ryori* (Buddhist temple cuisine), you have likely encountered goma tofu, a delightful sesame and kudzu starch delicacy, typically served cold. While sesame is the classic flavour, there are countless variations. This corn tofu is a personal summer favourite. I love how the natural sweetness of corn melds with the silky texture of the kudzu. Other variations I enjoy include yomogi (mugwort) tofu, tomato tofu and edamame tofu. Note that these dishes are called 'tofu' because their appearance and delicate texture resemble soybean tofu when served.

Kudzu is believed to promote circulation and relax tension in the body and is often used to help with early cold symptoms or muscle stiffness. When I feel a bit under the weather, I drink kudzu-yu – a mix of kudzu, grated ginger and hot water – before going to bed.

EQUIPMENT: Classic-style donabe (or heavy duty pot) (800 ml/27 fl oz), rectangular mould (I use one with a removable inner tray) (15 x 13.5 x 4 cm/6 x 5½ x 1¾ in) or similar-sized heatproof tin (pan)

METHOD: Slice the corn kernels off the cob. Blend the kernels with the water in a blender until very smooth. (I use a Vitamix for the smoothest result.)

Transfer the mixture to a donabe and add the salt and kudzu starch, whisking until the kudzu is fully dissolved. Set the donabe over a medium heat, stirring frequently with a spatula to prevent burning. Once the mixture begins to thicken, reduce the heat to medium-low to low and continue stirring for 8–10 minutes, or until the mixture becomes thick, pudding-like and glossy. You will notice a fragrant, sweetcorn aroma at this stage.

Remove from the heat and immediately pour into a rectangular mould. Let it cool for 10–15 minutes until the surface is dry enough to press lightly with a finger without sticking. For quicker cooling, place the mould in a water bath inside a deep tray.

Cover with cling film (plastic wrap) and refrigerate for 30 minutes–1 hour, or until fully set. It can be made up to a day in advance and kept chilled until ready to serve.

To serve, carefully lift the tray and turn it over to unmould and slice into 4–6 pieces. Garnish each piece with an okra slice, if using, and serve with a small dab of wasabi paste.

NOTE: Make sure to use pure kudzu starch such as authentic Japanese kudzu (hon-kuzu), so that the jelly can fully set and become a sliceable texture.

FLAVOUR VARIATION: For an edamame version, replace the corn with 250 g (8 oz) shelled, cooked edamame.

Corn Shira-Ae

CORN IN TOFU CREAM
とうもろこしの白和え

Serves 4

2 corn-on-the-cobs, cut in half
½–1 jalapeño, seeds removed and thinly sliced widthways (optional)
1 recipe quantity Shira-Ae Koromo (page 242)
handful of chopped fresh coriander (cilantro) or your choice of herbs

When corn is in season and at its sweetest, I often enjoy it simply steamed – no salt or seasoning needed. I love corn so much that this dish is really about celebrating the fresh flavour of the corn, tossed in the simple tofu cream. Every bite is naturally sweet, poppy and creamy. I like just these two components often, but the flavour is enhanced further with the addition of thinly sliced jalapeño and herbs.

EQUIPMENT: Donabe steamer (or pot with a steam basket)

METHOD: Set up the donabe steamer and bring the water to the boil. Arrange the corn on the grate, cover and steam over a medium-high heat for 4–5 minutes, or until just tender.

Let the corn cool slightly, then slice the kernels off the cob. Toss with the jalapeño (if using) and shira-ae koromo in a mixing bowl. Add the chopped herbs and toss again, then transfer to a serving bowl. Serve at room temperature or cool.

→ Plant-based small dishes: Zakkoku Gohan (page 170), Tofu Shiratama Miso Shiru (page 82), Corn Tofu (page 46), Shoga Hijiki (page 59), Mushi Nasu, Amazake Goma Miso Tare (page 50), Aka Cabbage Shio-Kombu Salad (page 43)

Mushi Nasu, Amazake Goma Miso Tare

STEAMED AUBERGINE WITH AMAZAKE SESAME MISO SAUCE

蒸しなすの
甘酒ごま味噌たれ

Serves 4

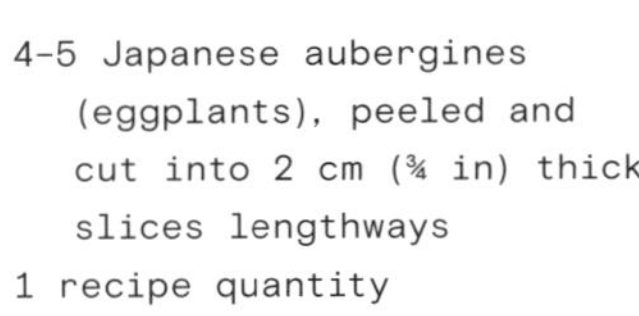

4–5 Japanese aubergines (eggplants), peeled and cut into 2 cm (¾ in) thick slices lengthways
1 recipe quantity Amazake Goma Miso Tare (page 242)
finely julienned shiso leaves, to garnish

Aubergine (eggplant) is an incredibly versatile ingredient and I love Japanese aubergine for its naturally sweet flavour and soft texture. I enjoy it steamed, grilled, sautéed, fried, simmered or even raw at times. When steamed without the skin, aubergine becomes exceptionally delicate, with a soft sweetness that melts in your mouth. Pairing it with the sesame sauce brings just the right balance of umami, nuttiness and natural sweetness.

EQUIPMENT: Donabe steamer (or pot with a steam basket)

METHOD: Set up the donabe steamer and bring the water to the boil. Arrange the aubergines on the grate (cut shorter, if needed), cover and steam over a medium-high heat for about 5–8 minutes, or until soft and cooked through. Transfer to a plate and let them cool to room temperature or chill in the refrigerator. The aubergines can be prepared up to a day ahead and stored in the refrigerator until you are ready to serve.

To serve, drain excess moisture from the aubergines, if necessary. Drizzle the aubergines with the amazake goma miso tare and garnish with the shiso leaves. Serve cool or chilled.

Satoimo no Tomo-Ae

TARO IN TARO SAUCE
里芋のともも和え

Serves 6

VG GF OP

700 g (1 lb 9 oz) satoimo (Japanese taro)
2 tbsp white sesame seeds
3 tbsp Saikyo miso or other sweet white miso
1 tbsp shiro shoyu (or 1 tsp sea salt for gluten free)
3–4 tbsp Shojin Dashi (page 233) or your choice of dashi (if using cold-infused dashi, bring it to the boil once so it's not raw)
pinch of sea salt, or to taste
grated zest of ½ lime

Satoimo (Japanese taro) is thought to support digestion and strengthen the immune system. I used to boil satoimo for this dish, but steaming it in a donabe steamer brings out its natural sweetness and makes peeling effortless. Steamed satoimo on its own is a simple yet traditional dish called kinukatsugi, typically enjoyed with just a sprinkle of salt or a dab of miso sauce. Tomo-ae refers to a dish dressed in a sauce made from the same ingredient, in this case, a velvety miso-sesame sauce mixed with mashed satoimo. The combination of its naturally sticky texture with the nutty sesame and mild sweetness of Saikyo miso is deeply comforting. I finish this dish with lime zest instead of traditional yuzu, adding a bright, refreshing note.

EQUIPMENT: Donabe steamer (or pot with a steam basket), large mortar and pestle (*suribachi* and *surikogi*), small pan or *horoku* (sesame roaster)

METHOD: Scrub the satoimo to remove excess hair, if necessary. If it's larger than 7–8 cm (3 in) in length, cut in half.

Set up the donabe steamer and bring the water to the boil. Arrange the satoimo on the grate, cover and steam over medium-high heat for 20–25 minutes, or until a skewer easily pierces the vegetable. Transfer to a basket or bowl and let cool until easy to handle. Peel the skins by hand.

Roast the sesame seeds in a small dry pan over a medium-low heat until aromatic. Transfer to a mortar and grind with the pestle, then add 1–2 pieces of satoimo and pound into a paste (it doesn't need to be completely smooth). If you don't have a large-enough mortar, use a potato masher to pound the satoimo in a bowl. Mix in the miso, shiro shoyu, dashi and a pinch of salt with a spatula until smooth. Adjust the consistency with more dashi, if desired, and season with more salt, if needed.

Add the remaining satoimo and mix to coat with the sauce. Transfer to a serving bowl and sprinkle with the lime zest. Serve warm or at room temperature.

NOTE: This dish is also great for obento (lunchboxes) or a picnic.

FLAVOUR VARIATION: A sprinkle of ground sansho brings a nice lift to the flavour.

Daikon Salad, Shio-Koji Dressing-Ae

DAIKON SALAD WITH SHIO-KOJI VINAIGRETTE

大根サラダの
塩麹ドレッシング和え

Serves 4

VG GF

240 g (8½ oz) daikon (mooli), peeled and julienned into 5 cm (2 in) lengths
½ watermelon radish, very thinly sliced
30 g (1 oz) radicchio, cut into thin strips
5 g (⅛ oz) dried mixed seaweed, rehydrated
2–3 tbsp roasted sliced almonds
Shio-Koji Dressing (page 243), to taste
daikon sprouts, to garnish

When I get a fresh, high-quality daikon radish (mooli), I love to make this salad. Daikon is often appreciated for its cooling properties and many people turn to it to ease a sore throat or cough.

The secret to its refreshing crunch is soaking the thinly sliced daikon in cold water – this simple step makes all the difference. I recommend using the upper part of the daikon, which is naturally sweeter, as the tip can have a wasabi-like kick. I like to pair it with radicchio for its slight bitterness, or aromatic vegetables like chrysanthemum leaves are also good, if you can find them. The mild, umami-rich shio-koji dressing enhances their flavours beautifully.

METHOD: Soak the daikon and watermelon radish in cold water for a few minutes, then drain well and pat dry with paper towel.

Combine the daikon, watermelon radish, radicchio, seaweed and almonds in a bowl. Add some shio-koji dressing and toss to coat evenly. Taste and add more shio-koji dressing, as needed.

Transfer to a serving bowl, top with daikon sprouts and serve immediately.

Kikurage Salad

WOOD EAR MUSHROOM AND CORIANDER SALAD

木耳と香菜のサラダ

Serves 4

For the salad

- 20 g (¾ oz) dried wood ear mushrooms
- 2 tbsp pine nuts
- 100 g (3½ oz) shelled, cooked edamame
- ½ tbsp very finely shredded fresh root ginger
- 20 g (¾ oz) fresh coriander (cilantro) leaves, very coarsely chopped
- shichimi togarashi (Japanese seven spice powder), to taste

For the kurozu sauce

- 3 tbsp kurozu (Japanese black vinegar) or rice vinegar
- 3 tbsp shoyu (or tamari for gluten free)
- 3 tbsp toasted sesame oil
- ½ tbsp raw brown sugar

Inspired by a popular Taiwanese appetiser, this dish highlights the bouncy texture of wood ear mushrooms, complemented by the deep, mellow notes of black vinegar and a bright kick of ginger. Dried wood ear mushrooms are thought to nourish and purifying the blood, supporting circulation and promoting healthy ageing, are a pantry staple for me – versatile and convenient for salads, soups and stir-fries.

METHOD: Soak the mushrooms in plenty of water for 30 minutes. Drain.

Whisk together all the ingredients for the sauce in a bowl and set aside.

Bring a saucepan of water to the boil and blanch the wood ear mushrooms for about 2 minutes. Drain and pat dry. Cut into bite-size pieces, discarding any gritty parts.

Preheat the oven to 180°C/350°F (160°C/320°F fan). Spread the pine nuts over a baking sheet and roast for about 7 minutes until lightly golden and fragrant.

Combine the mushrooms, pine nuts, edamame, ginger and coriander in a bowl. Drizzle with the sauce and toss well to coat.

Transfer to a serving bowl and sprinkle with shichimi togarashi. Serve cool or chilled.

This dish can be prepared a few hours ahead – just add the herbs right before serving for the best freshness.

Hakusai Asa-Zuke

QUICK-PICKLED NAPA CABBAGE IN SHIO-KOJI
白菜の浅漬け

Serves 4

240 g (8½ oz) napa cabbage, thinly sliced widthways
2 tbsp Shio-Koji (page 238)
½ tbsp very finely julienned fresh root ginger
1 tbsp pure yuzu juice or lemon juice
½ tbsp toasted sesame oil
½ tbsp toasted white sesame seeds

Asa-zuke, or quick pickles, are so easy to make and I enjoy them like a light, oil-free salad. Shio-koji adds a layer of umami, while ginger and yuzu bring a bright, citrussy character. This is great to serve with miso soup and rice or alongside a hearty main dish. Feel free to use different vegetables for shio-koji pickling – I also love using sliced kabu (Japanese turnip) and its leaves.

METHOD: Combine the napa cabbage and shio-koji in a large bowl and mix well by hand. Let stand for at least 30 minutes, or overnight.

Squeeze out the excess liquid from the cabbage. Add the ginger, yuzu juice, sesame oil and sesame seeds and mix well.

Transfer to a serving bowl and serve chilled or at room temperature.

Renkon Yuzu-Kosho Caper-Ae

LOTUS ROOT WITH YUZU-KOSHO CAPERS

蓮根の柚子胡椒
ケッパー和え

Serves 4

300 g (10½ oz) lotus root, very thinly sliced widthways
1 tbsp salted caperberries, rinsed thoroughly and patted dry
½ tsp yuzu-kosho (yuzu and green chilli pepper paste; see Note)
1 tsp rice vinegar
1 tbsp extra virgin olive oil, or more to taste
chopped coriander (cilantro), to garnish

This dish brings together Japanese and Mediterranean flavours in a way that always surprises people when they try it for the first time. The tender crunch of lotus root pairs beautifully with the bold, citrusy heat of yuzu-kosho, while caperberries and olive oil add a briny richness. I love serving it as a light, refreshing salad, but it's also delicious as a topping for a crusty slice of sourdough.

Hydrating lotus root is believed to sooth a dry throat or cough, while also promoting stamina and healthy ageing; when cooked, it becomes gentler on the stomach and helps improve digestion.

METHOD: Bring a saucepan of water to the boil, then add the lotus root and blanch for 2 minutes. Drain and pat dry with paper towel.

Coarsely chop the caperberries.

Whisk together the yuzu-kosho, vinegar and olive oil. Add the lotus root and caperberries, tossing to coat evenly. Transfer to a serving plate, sprinkle with the coriander and serve cool or chilled.

NOTES: I sometimes serve this alongside fish crudo. They make a great combo.

Yuzu-kosho is a bold, aromatic paste made from yuzu zest, fresh green or red chilli peppers and salt. The green variety is more common and known for its sharp citrus aroma and clean, spicy kick. Originally from the Kyushu region, just a small dab can brighten hotpots, sashimi, grilled food, salad or dipping sauces with layers of heat and fragrance.

Ruccola Salad, Shoga Miso Dressing-Ae

ROCKET SALAD WITH GINGER MISO VINAIGRETTE

ルッコラサラダの
味噌ドレッシング和え

Serves 4

60 g (2 oz) walnuts
150 g (5½ oz) shiitake mushrooms, stem ends removed, cut into 5 mm (¼ in) slices
1 tbsp extra virgin olive oil
100 g (3½ oz) rocket (arugula)
120 g (4 oz) red cabbage, finely shredded
1 persimmon, peeled, halved and cut into 5 mm (¼ in) slices
1 beetroot (beet), peeled, halved and cut into 2 mm (⅛ in) slices
1 quantity Shoga Miso Dressing (page 243)
sea salt and freshly ground black pepper, to taste

One of the biggest influences I have gained from LA food culture is a love for making big, colourful salads with a variety of fresh produce. I always enjoy visiting local farmers' markets and picking up whatever looks best. For this salad, I like to pair the peppery flavour of rocket (arugula) with a mix of ingredients and a bright, flavourful ginger miso vinaigrette. Feel free to switch up the ingredients – the measurements here are really just suggestions.

METHOD: Preheat the oven to 180°C/350°F (160°C/320°F fan).

Spread the walnuts on a baking sheet and roast for 7–8 minutes, or until lightly golden and fragrant.

Increase the oven temperature to 220°C/430°F (200°C/390°F fan). Toss the shiitake mushrooms with the olive oil and a pinch of salt, then spread them on a baking sheet. Roast for about 10 minutes, or until tender and slightly golden.

Combine the roasted walnuts, mushrooms, rocket, cabbage, persimmon and beetroot in a large bowl and toss with the shoga miso dressing. Adjust the seasoning with salt and black pepper, to taste.

Shoga Hijiki

QUICK-SIMMERED GINGER HIJIKI

生姜ひじき

Serves 4–6

- 30 g (1 oz) dried hijiki (seaweed)
- 120 ml (4 fl oz/½ cup) Shojin Dashi (page 233) or your choice of dashi
- 60 g (2 oz) fresh root ginger, very finely julienned
- 1½ tbsp mirin
- 1½ tbsp shoyu (or tamari for gluten free)

Seaweed is an essential part of Japanese cooking, and it's something I just can't live without. I love it so much that my pantry is always stocked with a variety of dried seaweeds: kombu, nori, aosa, funori, mekabu, tororo, mixed seaweed and more. Among them, hijiki is one of my absolute staples as it's incredibly versatile. This simple simmered hijiki with a generous amount of ginger is great on its own as a small side dish, mixed into salads or on top of rice. It's delicious at any temperature. Hijiki not only brings a unique texture and flavour to dishes but is also rich in minerals, including magnesium, iron and calcium. My mom used to tell me to eat more hijiki to keep my hair shiny and healthy for years to come.

EQUIPMENT: Classic-style donabe (or heavy duty pot) (1.2 litres/40 fl oz)

METHOD: Soak the hijiki in plenty of water for 30 minutes. Drain well.

Combine the dashi, ginger, mirin and shoyu in a donabe and bring to a simmer over a medium-high heat.

Add the hijiki, cover with a lid and bring to a high simmer, then reduce the heat to a low simmer and cook for about 10 minutes, or until most of the liquid has been absorbed.

Turn off the heat and let it rest for 15 minutes. Serve at any temperature.

NOTE: This dish is also great for obento (lunchboxes) or a picnic.

III

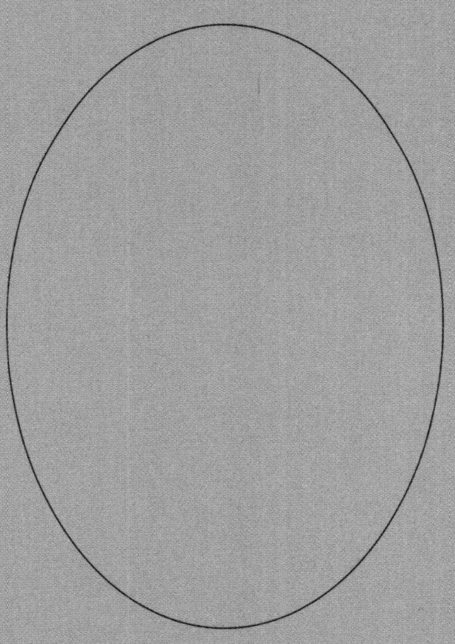

VEGETARIAN

It's all about simplicity. I love creating dishes that highlight the natural flavours and textures of vegetables, using a mixture of seasonal ingredients and everyday staples. In Japanese cooking, tofu has long been a primary source of protein, supporting health for centuries, and it remains at the core of many traditional meals. In addition to seasonal vegetables, mushrooms and seaweed are also essential parts of the Japanese diet. The recipes in this chapter are among my favourite vegetable-orientated mains prepared in donabe, where simple ingredients come together beautifully through gentle steaming, simmering or baking.

Iri Tofu

SIMMERED CRUMBLED TOFU AND VEGETABLES

炒り豆腐

Serves 2

 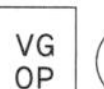 

- 00 g (10½ oz) medium-firm tofu
- 0 g (½ oz) dried wood ear mushrooms
- tbsp sesame oil
- tbsp finely shredded fresh root ginger
- tbsp water
- 0 ml (2 fl oz/¼ cup) Kaeshi (page 230)
- 00 g (3½ oz) carrot, julienned into 3 cm (1 in) lengths
- 00 g (3½ oz) shelled, cooked edamame
- large eggs
- ea salt, to taste
- spring onion (scallion), thinly sliced, to garnish
- round sansho (Japanese mountain pepper), to serve (optional)

A comforting and popular home-style Japanese dish, iri tofu is fluffy crumbled tofu simmered with vegetables. I like to use wood ear mushrooms, carrot and edamame for their balance of colour, flavour and texture. Sautéing the mushrooms in sesame oil first enhances the depth of flavour. While traditionally served warm, I also enjoy cold leftovers the next day.

Tofu is thought to be easy on the digestion and helps rebuild energy, while wood ear mushrooms are believed to support blood health and circulation. This dish is especially good for gently nourishing the body when dealing with chronic fatigue or low energy. I always feel more revitalised after eating it.

EQUIPMENT: Classic-style donabe (or heavy duty pot) (800 ml/27 fl oz)

METHOD: Place the tofu in a shallow tray and top with a flat tray or small cutting board. Add a weight 1–1.5 times the tofu's weight and let it sit for 30 minutes to remove excess moisture. Drain the liquid and pat the tofu dry with a paper towel.

Soak the wood ear mushrooms in plenty of water for 30 minutes. Drain, rinse well and squeeze out excess moisture. Cut the mushrooms into thin shreds, discarding any gritty parts.

Heat the sesame oil in a donabe over a medium heat. Add the mushrooms and ginger, and sauté until fragrant, about 1 minute.

Crumble the tofu into the donabe by hand, squeezing gently, and sauté for another minute.

Add the water and kaeshi, followed by the carrot. Cover and simmer for 6–8 minutes, or until most of the liquid has been absorbed. Stir in the edamame.

Whisk the eggs with a pinch of salt, then drizzle into the donabe, cover and turn off the heat. Let stand for 1–2 minutes until the eggs are halfway set but still slightly soft. Uncover and gently stir the mixture so the eggs fully incorporate with the tofu and vegetables, creating a soft, fluffy texture. Adjust the seasoning with more salt, if needed.

Garnish with the spring onion and sprinkle with some ground sansho, if desired.

NOTE: For a vegan version, simply omit the eggs. My grandma made hers this way, and I loved it so much!

Shoyu-Koji Sukiyaki

SHOYU-KOJI SUKIYAKI WITH TWO KINDS OF TOFU

醤油麹すき焼き

Serves 2–3

For the warishita (sukiyaki sauce)

- 120 ml (4 fl oz/½ cup) Shojin Dashi (page 233) or your choice of dashi
- 60 ml (2 fl oz/¼ cup) mirin
- 60 ml (2 fl oz/¼ cup) tamari

For the donabe

- 1 tbsp sesame oil
- 3 spring onions (scallions) (white parts only, cut into 4 cm/1½ in pieces and halved lengthways; reserve green tops for garnish)
- ½ tbsp finely julienned fresh root ginger
- 120 g (4 oz) king oyster mushrooms, diced
- 100 g (3½ oz) soft yuba (tofu skin), cut into strips
- ½ courgette (zucchini), cut into 3 mm (⅛ in) thick half-moon slices
- 1 x 400 g (14 oz) package medium-firm tofu, cut into bite-size pieces
- 4 tsp Okinawa black sugar or raw brown sugar
- 4 tsp Kombu Shoyu-Koji (page 237), or more to taste

To serve

- chopped fresh coriander (cilantro)
- reserved spring onion tops, thinly sliced
- ground sansho (Japanese mountain pepper)

Sukiyaki isn't just for meat – this plant-based version is surprisingly rich and deeply satisfying. I love combining two kinds of tofu – medium-firm tofu and soft yuba – with a variety of vegetables, but you can use any ingredients you like. Adding Kombu Shoyu-Koji (page 237) towards the end enhances the umami and deepens the sauce's flavour. Serve it over rice for a comforting sukiyaki-don (sukiyaki rice bowl)!

EQUIPMENT: Classic-style donabe (or heavy duty pot) (1.8 litre/60 fl oz)

METHOD: Combine the ingredients for the warishita and set aside.

Heat the sesame oil in a donabe over a medium heat. Add the spring onion whites and ginger, and sauté for a couple of minutes until aromatic.

Add the mushrooms, yuba, courgette and tofu, arranging them neatly in the donabe. Sprinkle the sugar over the top and pour in the warishita. Increase the heat to medium-high, cover and bring to a high simmer.

Add the kombu shoyu-koji, cover again and reduce the heat to a low simmer. Cook for 2–3 minutes.

Serve in individual bowls, garnished with coriander and the reserved spring onion greens, and sprinkled with ground sansho.

FLAVOUR VARIATION: Instead of yuba, tofu shirataki or regular shirataki (konnyaku) noodles can be used for a different texture – they soak up the sukiyaki sauce beautifully and taste great.

Shirataki Ninjin Shiri Shiri

SHIRATAKI AND CARROT WITH SOFT-COOKED EGG

白滝と人参のしりしり

Serves 2

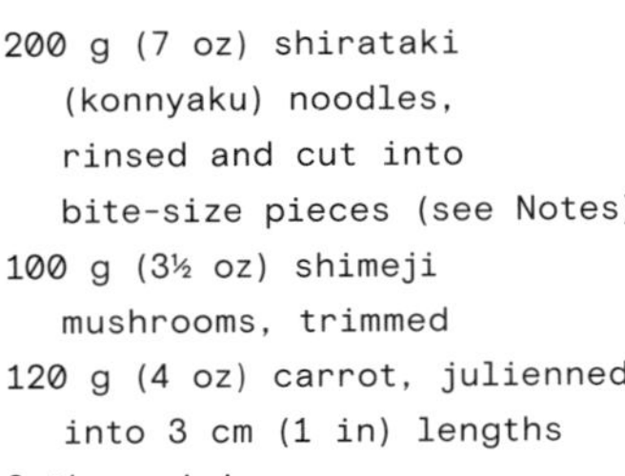

- 200 g (7 oz) shirataki (konnyaku) noodles, rinsed and cut into bite-size pieces (see Notes)
- 100 g (3½ oz) shimeji mushrooms, trimmed
- 120 g (4 oz) carrot, julienned into 3 cm (1 in) lengths
- 2 tbsp mirin
- 1 tbsp shoyu (or tamari for gluten free)
- ½ tsp sea salt
- 1 tbsp toasted sesame oil
- 2 large eggs
- 2 tbsp toasted white sesame seeds
- pure sudachi citrus juice (see Notes) (or other citrus, such as yuzu or Meyer lemon), to serve

This is my twist on Okinawa's classic *shiri shiri* (grated carrot stir-fry with egg). Shirataki (konnyaku) noodles and shimeji mushrooms add body to a light but satisfying one-pot dish. I julienne the carrot for a more substantial texture and layer all the ingredients directly into the donabe to gently steam and simmer together. It's an easy dish to whip up with staples I usually have in the refrigerator. I finish it by stirring in eggs while still hot for a soft, crumbled finish. A splash of fresh sudachi citrus juice adds a bright touch.

EQUIPMENT: Classic-style donabe (or heavy duty pot) (1.2 litre/40 fl oz)

METHOD: Spread the shirataki in the base of a donabe and layer the mushrooms and carrot on top. Cover with the lid and set over a medium heat. Once the vegetables release moisture and begin to simmer, continue to cook for about 2 minutes.

Add the mirin, shoyu and salt. Cover again and simmer until most of the liquid has been absorbed, about 10 minutes.

Drizzle in the sesame oil and stir gently. Make a small well in the middle and crack in the eggs. Cover and cook for 2 minutes, just until the outer sides of the eggs start to set.

Turn off the heat and gently stir to break the eggs and mix them with the other ingredients – the residual heat will finish cooking them to a soft, crumbly texture. Stir in the sesame seeds.

Serve warm with a splash of fresh sudachi juice.

NOTES: If you find the earthy aroma of shirataki (konnyaku) noodles too strong, you can blanch them in boiling water for about 2 minutes before cutting.

For a vegan option, simply omit the eggs. This tastes great without them, too!

Sudachi is a small, green, aromatic and sour citrus native to Japan. You can also find it in a bottle at speciality stores outside of Japan. Feel free to switch to your choice of other citrus or omit if you prefer.

FLAVOUR VARIATION: Add a pinch of shichimi togarashi or ground sansho at the end for a spicy or peppery finish.

Furofuki Daikon

SIMMERED DAIKON WITH MISO SAUCE

風呂吹き大根

Serves 3–4

For the miso sauce

5 tbsp Saikyo miso
3 tbsp miso
2 tbsp mirin
1 tsp pure yuzu juice or rice vinegar

For the simmered daikon soup

1 daikon (mooli) (about 800 g/1 lb 12 oz)
1 litre (34 fl oz/4¼ cups) Shojin Dashi (page 233) or your choice of dashi
2 tsp sea salt
10 g (½ oz) dried wakame, rehydrated and cut into bite-size pieces, if needed

To serve

very finely julienned yuzu zest (optional)

Tender daikon (mooli) simmered in dashi broth and topped with a slightly sweet, rich miso sauce is a classic in Japanese cooking. Steaming the daikon first may seem like an extra step, but it makes all the difference – it helps the daikon absorb the broth beautifully and gives it an extra-tender texture. Letting it rest in the broth is also key. I enjoy taking time and care with this simple dish, and it's absolutely worth it. You can also add mushrooms or other vegetables to the broth to make it a more complete meal.

Daikon is thought to promote healthy digestion, ease bloating and clear excess heat, helping to soothe the throat and chest. Miso is said to support fluid balance and help calm irritation and swelling, while wakame is believed to gently nourish the body and support natural detox. This simple dish always makes me feel clean and refreshed from the inside.

EQUIPMENT: Classic-style donabe (or heavy duty pot) (1.8 litre/60 fl oz)

METHOD: Whisk together all the miso sauce ingredients, except the yuzu juice, in a small saucepan. Cook over a moderate heat, stirring frequently with a spatula, until smooth and glossy, about 3–5 minutes. Add the yuzu juice and stir for 30 seconds, then turn off the heat. Reheat before serving.

Peel the daikon slightly thicker than usual, as the outer layer tends to be fibrous. Cut into 4 cm (1½ in) thick rounds and bevel the edges of each piece – this step is optional, but makes the daikon look prettier and helps prevent the edges from breaking during cooking. Score an X on one side of each piece, about 1 cm (½ in) deep, to help it absorb the dashi flavour.

Set up the donabe steamer and bring the water to the boil. Arrange the daikon on the grate. Cover and steam over a medium-high heat for 25–30 minutes, or until a skewer easily pierces through.

Bring the dashi to a simmer in a separate donabe and add the salt. Carefully transfer the steamed daikon to the dashi and simmer gently for 10–15 minutes. Turn off the heat and let it rest for 30 minutes–1 hour.

Bring the soup back to a gentle simmer and add the wakame, then turn off the heat.

To serve, divide the daikon and wakame among individual bowls. Top each daikon with a generous dab of miso sauce and pour some of the dashi from the side. Serve with yuzu zest on top of the miso sauce, if desired.

NOTE: The yuzu-scented miso sauce is versatile. You can also use it as a dipping sauce for crudités or steamed vegetables. I often mix any leftover sauce with olive oil to make a quick dressing.

Shojin Tōnyu Nabe

TEMPLE-STYLE TOFU HOTPOT IN SOYA MILK BROTH

精進豆乳鍋

Serves 4

- 6 medium leaves of napa cabbage, cut into bite-size pieces
- 15 g (½ oz) dried white wood ear mushrooms, rehydrated and bottom ends trimmed
- 200 g (7 oz) medium-firm tofu, cut into large bite-size pieces
- ½ tbsp finely julienned fresh root ginger
- 150 g (5½ oz) nagaimo (Japanese mountain yam), peeled, cut into 6 mm (¼ in) rounds and quartered
- 300 ml (10 fl oz/1¼ cups) Shojin Dashi (page 233) or your choice of dashi
- 60 ml (2 fl oz/¼ cup) sake
- ½ tsp baking powder
- 4 tbsp Saikyo miso or other sweet white miso
- 1 tbsp shiro shoyu (can substitute 1 tsp sea salt for gluten free)
- 300 ml (10 fl oz/1¼ cups) pure soya milk
- sea salt, to taste
- 60 g (2 oz) mizuna (mustard greens) or your choice of leafy green, chopped
- toasted white sesame seeds, ground, to serve

This comforting hotpot brings together delicate white ingredients like napa cabbage, tofu, white wood ear mushrooms and nagaimo (Japanese mountain yam) in a creamy soya-milk broth. To keep the broth smooth and prevent curdling, I add a small amount of baking powder before stirring in the soya milk – a simple trick that makes the tofu extra soft.

EQUIPMENT: Classic-style donabe (or heavy duty pot) (1.8 litre/60 fl oz)

METHOD: Combine the cabbage, mushrooms, tofu, ginger, nagaimo, dashi and sake in a donabe. Set over a medium-high heat and bring to the boil, then reduce to a simmer and cook for 5 minutes.

Add the baking powder (it might bubble up slightly, so watch carefully), then whisk in the miso and shiro shoyu. If the miso is firm, ladle some of the soup into a small bowl with the miso, whisk until smooth, then pour it back into the donabe. Adjust the seasoning with salt, if needed.

Add the soya milk and bring back to a simmer. Cook for 2–3 minutes, then add the mizuna and turn off the heat. Let the mizuna wilt, then serve in individual bowls. Generously sprinkle with ground sesame seeds and enjoy.

Yuba Daikon Mille-Feuille Nabe

LAYERED TOFU SKIN AND DAIKON HOTPOT

湯葉と大根のミルフィーユ鍋

Serves 4

- 6 tbsp miso (lighter-coloured miso is preferred)
- 400 ml (14 fl oz/generous 1½ cups) Shojin Dashi (page 233) or your choice of dashi
- 2 tbsp sake
- 450 g (1 lb) napa cabbage
- 350 g (12 oz) daikon, cut into 3 mm (⅛ in) thick rounds
- 150 g (5½ oz) soft yuba (tofu skin), cut into 5 cm (2 in) wide strips
- 1 tbsp very finely julienned fresh root ginger
- 2 garlic cloves, thinly sliced
- 4 shiitake mushrooms, trimmed and thinly sliced
- chopped chives and coriander (cilantro), to garnish
- yuzu zest and ½ yuzu, to garnish
- yuzu-kosho (yuzu and green chilli pepper paste), to serve (optional)

The mille-feuille nabe has become a popular hotpot in Japan for its beautiful layers and easy preparation. This plant-based version swaps pork belly for yuba (tofu skin) and daikon (mooli), creating a rich, nourishing dish that always makes my body feel good. I love using miso for its deep, savoury notes and finishing with yuzu-kosho for a bright, citrussy accent. As the layers gently simmer, they soak up the flavourful broth, making each bite comforting and satisfying. For a non-vegan variation, I sometimes add shelled oysters a few minutes before finishing cooking – it's delicious!

EQUIPMENT: Classic-style donabe (or heavy duty pot) (1.8 litre/60 fl oz)

METHOD: Whisk together the miso, dashi and sake in a bowl.

Place a napa cabbage leaf on a cutting board. Arrange a few daikon rounds over the cabbage, then top with a strip of yuba. Repeat the layering two more times, finishing with a layer of napa cabbage. Set aside. Repeat the process with the remaining ingredients.

Cut each layered set into 5 cm (2 in) wide pieces, then tightly arrange them in the donabe, starting from the outer edge. Pour in the miso broth and evenly distribute the ginger, garlic and shiitake mushrooms on top.

Cover and set over a medium-high heat. Bring to the boil, then reduce to a gentle simmer and cook for 20 minutes, or until everything is cooked through and the napa cabbage is very tender.

Garnish with chopped chives, coriander and yuzu zest. Squeeze yuzu juice, if using. Serve in individual bowls and enjoy with yuzu-kosho on the side, if desired.

Kabocha no Itoko-Ni

KABOCHA AND ADZUKI STEW
南瓜のいとこ煮

Serves 4

- 400 g (14 oz) kabocha squash, cut into 3-4 cm (1.5 in) square pieces
- 120 g (4 oz) dried adzuki beans, rinsed
- water, as needed
- 3 tbsp raw brown sugar
- 2 tbsp sake
- 1 tbsp shiro shoyu
- sea salt, to taste

Itoko-ni is a comforting dish rooted in *shojin ryori* (Buddhist temple cuisine) and often made during the coldest months to warm the body. The name is a playful reference to slowly simmering ingredients in stages, like 'cousins cooking together'. Kabocha squash and adzuki beans are one of my favourite combinations, and the donabe brings out their natural sweetness beautifully. I've been making this dish for decades, and it's one I never get tired of.

EQUIPMENT: Classic-style donabe (or heavy duty pot) (1.8 litre/60 fl oz)

METHOD: To prepare the kabocha, shave off any rough brown parts on the skin and bevel the edges of each piece (skin side) – this step is optional, but makes the kabocha look prettier and helps prevent the edges from breaking during cooking.

To prepare the adzuki beans, place them in a donabe with plenty of water and bring to the boil. Boil for about 3 minutes, then drain. Add the drained adzuki back to the donabe with about 600 ml (20 fl oz/2½ cups) fresh water and bring to the boil again. Reduce the heat to a gentle simmer and cook for 1–1½ hours until the beans are tender. Check and stir a few times after 30 minutes, and add more water, if needed. The beans should be submerged just under the water when ready.

Arrange the kabocha, skin-side down, in a single layer over the adzuki in the donabe. Add the sugar, sake and shiro shoyu. Place a drop lid or baking parchment cartouche directly on the surface of the kabocha to help the ingredients absorb the flavours evenly. Bring to a high simmer over a medium-high heat, then reduce to a gentle simmer. Cook for 15–20 minutes, or until the kabocha is tender. Adjust the seasoning with salt, if needed. Turn off the heat and leave to rest for 15–20 minutes.

Serve warm or at room temperature.

NOTES: For a gluten-free version, replace the shiro shoyu with 1 teaspoon tamari and ½ teaspoon sea salt or more to taste. The colour will be darker, but the flavour won't be compromised.

Placing a piece of parchment cartouche directly on the surface of the ingredients is a useful technique when the liquid doesn't fully cover them. It helps circulate the cooking liquid evenly and encourages better absorption of flavour. In Japanese cooking, we often use a drop lid called *otoshibuta* for this purpose. If you have one, you can use it in place of the parchment.

Mushi Daikon Mochi

STEAMED DAIKON CAKE
蒸し大根餅

Serves 2

300 g (10½ oz) daikon (mooli), cut into thin rounds, then into thin strips
100 g (3½ oz) enoki mushrooms, trimmed and halved
1 small carrot, thinly cut at an angle, then into thin strips
½ tbsp finely julienned fresh root ginger
½ tsp sea salt
Freshly ground white pepper or black pepper, to taste
1 tbsp katakuriko (potato starch)
Sesame oil, for greasing

To serve

La-yu (chilli oil) or chilli crunch
Fresh coriander (cilantro) leaves
Shoyu (or tamari for gluten free)
Rice vinegar

Daikon (mooli) is such a versatile ingredient – I enjoy it both raw and cooked. This dish was inspired by dim sum-style daikon cake, and instead of the classic pan-fried version made with rice flour, it's steamed for a lighter texture and more pure flavour. Shredded daikon, enoki mushrooms and carrot are mixed with katakuriko (potato starch) and steamed until soft and mochi-like in texture. It's quick to make, satisfying yet gentle on the stomach, and I love serving it with a drizzle of la-yu (chilli oil) or chilli crunch. It serves two as part of a meal, but I often make it just for myself and end up finishing the whole thing.

EQUIPMENT: Donabe steamer (or pot with a steam basket), heatproof shallow bowl (about 20 cm/8 in in diameter)

METHOD: Set up the donabe steamer and bring the water to a boil.

Mix all the ingredients (except the sesame oil) quickly in a bowl by hand. Don't let the mixture sit, as the salt will draw out moisture from the daikon and make it watery.

Lightly coat the heatproof bowl with sesame oil and spread the mixture evenly into it. Place the bowl on the steam grate of the donabe, cover and steam over a medium-high heat for 10–12 minutes, or until everything is cooked and soft.

To serve, drizzle with la-yu and garnish with coriander leaves.

For a dipping sauce, each person can mix shoyu and rice vinegar to their taste in a small saucer (I like a 1:1 ratio). Break the daikon cake with chopsticks or a spoon and enjoy with the sauce.

FLAVOUR VARIATION: For a non-vegetarian option, I like adding sakura-ebi (dried shrimp) to the mixture to steam.

Tofu Shiratama Miso-Shiru

TOFU DUMPLING AND BRUSSELS SPROUTS MISO SOUP

豆腐白玉のお味噌汁

Serves 4

90 g (3¼ oz/scant ¾ cup) shiratamako (glutinous rice flour)
110–130 g (3¾–4½ oz) silken tofu
1 tbsp extra virgin olive oil
250 g (9 oz) Brussels sprouts, halved or quartered if large
150 g (5½ oz) shimeji mushrooms, trimmed
800 ml (27 fl oz/3¼ cups) Shojin Dashi (page 233) or your choice of dashi
120 ml (4 fl oz/½ cup) Saikyo miso or other sweet white miso
toasted sesame seeds, ground, to serve

This lightly creamy soup is seasoned with Saikyo miso, a sweet, delicate miso from Kyoto, and filled with sautéed Brussels sprouts and soft dumplings made with shiratamako (glutinous rice flour) and silken tofu instead of water. The tofu gives the dumplings an extra fluffy texture and makes them lighter, too. It's a comforting, nourishing bowl that I love to make when I want something easy and satisfying.

EQUIPMENT: Classic-style donabe (or heavy duty pot) (1.8 litre/60 fl oz)

METHOD: To make the tofu dumplings, knead together the shiratamako with 110 g (3¾ oz) of the tofu by hand. If the mixture feels a bit dry, add more tofu, a little at a time. Knead until the texture is soft but not wet – almost like play-dough. Roll into 12 balls by hand. Cover and set aside.

Heat the olive oil in a donabe over a medium-high heat. Add the sprouts and sauté for about 1 minute until evenly coated in oil. Add the mushrooms and continue to sauté for another minute. Pour in the dashi and bring to a high simmer.

Gently reshape the dumplings before adding them to the soup. Cook for 3–4 minutes.

Dissolve the miso thoroughly in the soup. If the miso is firm, ladle some of the soup into a small bowl with the miso, whisk until smooth, then pour it back into the donabe.

Serve in individual bowls, generously sprinkled with ground sesame seeds, and enjoy.

Yuba and Asparagus Tamago-Toji

SIMMERED TOFU SKIN AND ASPARAGUS WITH EGG IN DASHI

湯葉とアスパラガスの卵とじ

Serves 2

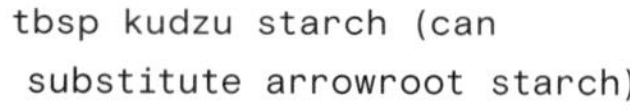

- 1 tbsp kudzu starch (can substitute arrowroot starch)
- 2 tbsp water
- 240 ml (8 fl oz/1 cup) Shojin Dashi (page 233) or your choice of dashi
- 2 tbsp mirin
- 2 tbsp shoyu (or tamari for gluten free)
- ½ tbsp finely julienned fresh root ginger
- 75 g (2½ oz) soft yuba (tofu skin), cut into bite-size pieces (or 150 g/5½ oz silken tofu, uncut)
- 100 g (3½ oz) shimeji mushrooms, trimmed
- 80 g (2¾ oz) asparagus, woody ends trimmed and cut into 1 cm (½ in) lengths
- 3 large eggs, beaten
- chopped mitsuba (Japanese parsley) or chives, to garnish
- ground sansho (Japanese mountain pepper), to serve (optional)

This dish is somewhere between a soup and a stew, with silky yuba (tofu skin) and a soothing broth slightly thickened with kudzu starch. The base of the dish is *happo dashi* – a golden ratio of dashi, mirin and shoyu (8:1:1). It's one of my favourite foundations in Japanese cooking, as it allows for endless variations. The gentle heat of ginger and the soft-set egg bring warmth and comfort to every bite. It comes together quickly in a small donabe. I especially love serving it over a bowl of rice to make it a satisfying donburi dish, rather than serving the rice on the side.

Eggs are thought to help replenish fluids, restore energy and calm the mind, while asparagus are believed to support kidney health, promote gentle detox and cool internal heat. Together, they make this dish especially good for relaxation and better sleep. That's why I actually enjoy eating eggs more for dinner than for breakfast!

EQUIPMENT: Classic-style donabe (or heavy duty pot) (800 ml/27 fl oz)

METHOD: Stir together the kudzu starch with the water in a small cup and set aside.

Combine the dashi, mirin and shoyu in a donabe and bring to a high simmer over a medium-high heat. Add the ginger, yuba (if using silken tofu, scoop small pieces with a spoon) and mushrooms, and bring back to a high simmer. Stir the kudzu solution again, then gently stir into the broth to thicken.

Add the asparagus and simmer for about 1 minute, then slowly drizzle in the beaten eggs in a circular motion. Cover and let it cook for about 1 minute, then turn off the heat. Let the eggs continue to cook in the residual heat for another 1–2 minutes to your preferred consistency.

Garnish with mitsuba and sprinkle with sansho, if desired.

FLAVOUR VARIATION: Instead of asparagus, broad (fava) beans, broccoli rabe (rapini) (both blanched before adding) or garden peas can work great also, as they go really well with fluffy eggs. Adjust the cooking times according to your liking.

Onishime

SIMMERED JAPANESE ROOT VEGETABLES

お煮しめ

Serves 4

- 4 dried shiitake mushrooms, quickly rinsed
- 250 ml (8 fl oz/1 cup) water
- 1 x 250 g (9 oz) block konnyaku (yam cake)
- 300 g (10½ oz) satoimo (Japanese taro)
- 50 g (1¾ oz) mangetout (snow peas), trimmed and side string removed
- 2 tbsp sesame oil
- 150 g (5½ oz) burdock root, cut into bite-size pieces on the diagonal
- 250 g (9 oz) lotus root, cut into bite-size pieces on the diagonal
- 60 ml (2 fl oz/¼ cup) sake
- 1 tbsp Okinawa black sugar or raw brown sugar
- 1 tbsp mirin
- 2 tbsp usukuchi shoyu (can substitute ½ tbsp sea salt for gluten free)
- 1 tbsp shoyu (or tamari for gluten free)
- 1 carrot, cut into bite-size pieces on the diagonal
- shichimi togarashi (Japanese seven spice powder), to serve (optional)

Originating in shojin ryori (Buddhist temple cuisine), onishime highlights simmered earthy root vegetables and natural umami. The dish becomes even more comforting as it rests, with the flavours deepening overnight. While this version is plant-based, I also sometimes add cut chicken thighs for a heartier variation.

Konnyaku, made from the starchy root of the konjac plant, is a Japanese staple. I love its bouncy texture so much. It's often called a 'broom for the intestines' in Japan, and is thought to promote digestive health with its high fibre content.

EQUIPMENT: Classic-style donabe (or heavy duty pot) (1.8 litre/60 fl oz)

METHOD: Soak the dried shiitake in the water for about 2 hours or until fully rehydrated and aromatic (if you are in a rush, use hot water and soak for about 30 minutes). Trim the stems and cut each mushroom in half. Reserve 180 ml (6 fl oz/¾ cup) of the soaking water.

To prepare the twisted konnyaku, cut it into 5 mm (¼ in) thick strips widthways. Make a 1.5 cm (¾ in) cut lengthways in the centre of each piece, then push one end into the slit to make a knot. Bring a saucepan of water to the boil, add the konnyaku and blanch for 2–3 minutes. Drain.

To prepare the satoimo, peel and cut in half or into large bite-size pieces. Place in a saucepan with enough water to cover. Bring to the boil, then reduce to a simmer and blanch for 2–3 minutes. Drain. This process helps remove excess sliminess and prevents the stew from becoming foamy during cooking.

To prepare the mangetout, bring a pan of water to the boil and blanch the mangetout for 30 seconds. Drain and immediately transfer to a bowl of iced water to retain their bright colour. Drain again and pat dry with paper towel.

Heat the sesame oil in a donabe over a medium-high heat. Add the shiitake, konnyaku, burdock root and lotus root, and sauté for a couple of minutes. Add the sake, sugar and mirin, and continue to cook until the liquid is reduced, about 3–5 minutes.

Pour in the reserved shiitake soaking water, usukuchi shoyu and shoyu Place a drop lid or baking parchment cartouche directly on the surface of the ingredients to help the broth circulate evenly. Bring to the boil, then reduce to a simmer and cook for 10–15 minutes, or until the broth is reduced by about one-third.

Add the satoimo and carrot, and continue to cook for another 7–10 minutes, or until most of the liquid has been absorbed. Turn off the heat and let it rest for 10–15 minutes or longer, allowing the flavours to meld

Arrange the mangetout neatly on top. Serve warm or at room temperature with a sprinkle of shichimi togarashi, if desired.

Nanohana Curry

BROCCOLI RABE CURRY
菜の花カレー

Serves 4

For the sauce

300 g (10½ oz) broccoli rabe (rapini)
1 x 400 ml (14 fl oz) can unsweetened coconut milk
2 tbsp Shio-Koji (page 238)
2 umeboshi (pickled plums), pitted, or 1 tbsp umeboshi paste

For the donabe

2 tbsp extra virgin olive oil
1 garlic clove, finely grated
1 tsp finely grated fresh root ginger
½ tsp cumin seeds
1 tbsp curry powder
150 g (5½ oz) cauliflower, cut into bite-size pieces
1 x 400 g (14 oz) can chickpeas (garbanzos), drained
1 bay leaf
180 ml (6 fl oz/¾ cup) Shojin Dashi (page 233) or vegetable stock
150 g (5½ oz) okra, top end trimmed and cut into 1 cm (½ in) pieces
a large handful of mixed herbs (such as coriander/cilantro, mint, basil, and/or parsley), chopped
sea salt and freshly ground black pepper, to taste

To serve

coconut yoghurt
garam masala

I love broccoli rabe (rapini) so much that I wanted to turn it into a vibrant green curry, and it worked beautifully. The slight bitterness of the vegetable blends perfectly with the sweetness of coconut milk, the umami of shio-koji and a touch of brightness from umeboshi plums (my secret ingredient). The sauce is rich yet fresh, and when cooked with ingredients like chickpeas (garbanzos), cauliflower, mushrooms and okra, it becomes a hearty, satisfying stew, perfect for a spring reset. I like to serve it with Orange Saffron Rice (page 198) or short pasta.

EQUIPMENT: Classic-style donabe (or heavy duty pot) (1.8 litre/60 fl oz)

METHOD: To prepare the sauce, bring a saucepan of water to the boil. Blanch the broccoli rabe for 1 minute, then drain and immediately transfer to a bowl of iced water to preserve its bright colour. Drain again and gently squeeze out excess moisture. Cut into 3 cm (1 in) pieces.

Combine three-quarters of the broccoli rabe in a blender (I like to use a Vitamix) with the coconut milk, shio-koji and umeboshi. Blend until smooth.

Heat the olive oil in a donabe over a medium heat. Add the garlic, ginger, cumin and curry powder, and sauté for 1 minute, or until aromatic. Add the cauliflower and chickpeas and stir well, then add the bay leaf. Pour in the dashi, cover and bring to a simmer. Cook for 5–10 minutes, or until the liquid is reduced by half.

Stir in the sauce and okra. Bring back to a simmer and adjust the seasoning with salt and pepper, if needed. Stir in the mixed herbs and remaining broccoli rabe.

Serve in individual bowls with a small scoop of yoghurt and a sprinkle of garam masala on top. Serve on its own or with freshly cooked rice or short pasta, if desired.

FLAVOUR VARIATION: This curry is also good with meat or seafood. I sometimes add prawns (shrimp) to cook in the sauce.

Kanzuri Shakshuka

VEGETABLE AND MUSHROOM SHAKSHUKA WITH SPICY CHERRY TOMATO SAUCE

かんずりシャクシューカ

Serves 2–4

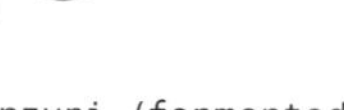

- 2 tbsp kanzuri (fermented chilli and yuzu paste)
- 2 tbsp sake
- 2 tbsp coconut yoghurt or Greek-style yoghurt
- 1 tbsp extra virgin olive oil
- 350 g (12 oz) satsumaimo (Japanese sweet potato), cut into 1 cm (½ in) dice
- 150 g (5½ oz) king oyster mushrooms, cut into 1 cm (½ in) dice
- 2 garlic cloves, thinly sliced
- 1 tsp cumin seeds
- 200 g (7 oz) baby spinach
- 1 x 400 g (14 oz) can cherry tomatoes
- 4 tbsp water
- 1 tbsp Shio-Koji (page 238)
- 40 g (1½ oz/¼ cup) garden peas
- 4 large eggs
- freshly ground black pepper, to taste
- chopped parsley, to garnish

I love anything with eggs, and this donabe shakshuka has become one of my favourite easy meals when I'm craving something hearty and comforting. The sauce is seasoned with kanzuri – a fermented chilli and yuzu paste from Niigata, which adds a gentle heat and deep umami to the rich tomatoes. Japanese sweet potato, mushrooms, spinach and peas add layers of texture and make the dish extra satisfying.

EQUIPMENT: Tagine-style donabe (or frying pan/skillet with a lid)

METHOD: To make the kanzuri-sake mixture, stir together 1 tablespoon of the kanzuri with the sake in a small bowl.

To make the kanzuri-yoghurt sauce, mix the remaining tablespoon of kanzuri with the yoghurt in a separate bowl.

Preheat the oven to 230°C/450°F (210°C/410°F fan).

Add the olive oil, satsumaimo, mushrooms and garlic to a donabe. Cover and set over a medium heat. Cook for 5–7 minutes, stirring occasionally, until the satsumaimo is lightly golden and almost tender.

Uncover, add the cumin seeds and spinach, and sauté for another 2 minutes. Stir in the kanzuri-sake mixture.

Add the cherry tomatoes, then the water (rinse out the empty tomato can with the water before pouring it into the donabe), then the shio-koji and some black pepper. Bring to a simmer and cook for 2–3 minutes.

Stir in the peas, then turn off the heat.

Crack one egg at a time into a small cup. Make a small indentation in the tomato mixture and gently slide the egg into it. Repeat with the remaining eggs, spacing them evenly.

Transfer the donabe to the oven and bake, uncovered, for 12–13 minutes until the eggs are softly set to your liking.

Garnish with dabs of kanzuri-yoghurt sauce and chopped parsley before serving.

NOTE: For a vegan version, simply omit the eggs. It's still hearty and delicious even without them.

Lentil Daikon Miso-Shiru

LENTIL AND DAIKON MISO SOUP

レンズ豆と大根のお味噌汁

Serves 4

For the donabe

2 medium napa cabbage leaves, cut into small bite-size pieces
100 g (3½ oz) enoki mushrooms, trimmed, cut into 3 cm (1 in) lengths
150 g (5½ oz) daikon (mooli), cut into 3 mm (⅛ in) rounds and further cut into halves or quarters, depending on size
250 g (9 oz/1 cup) mixture of dried red and yellow lentils or either kind, rinsed
1 litre (34 fl oz/4¼ cups) Shojin Dashi (page 233) or vegetable stock
5 tbsp miso
sea salt, to taste

For the sesame Tenderstem broccoli

100 g (3½ oz) Tenderstem broccoli (broccolini)
1 tbsp toasted and ground white sesame seeds, or more to taste
1 tsp Shio-Koji (page 238) (or a good pinch of sea salt)
extra virgin olive oil, for drizzling

Miso soup is at the heart of everyday meals for me, and I often make it with whatever I have on hand. I love Western-style lentil soup, too, so I started cooking lentils with dashi and found they pair beautifully with tender daikon (mooli). This soup is so simple – just simmer everything together and finish with good miso. Homemade dashi is always ideal, but sometimes I use a good store-bought vegetable stock for a change, and it works great here. Topping it with sesame-dusted Tenderstem broccoli (broccolini) adds a fresh, satisfying touch and makes it feel like a complete meal.

EQUIPMENT: Classic-style donabe (or heavy duty pot) (1.8 litre/60 fl oz)

METHOD: To make the miso soup, pile the cabbage, mushrooms, daikon and lentils into a donabe. Pour in the dashi, cover, and set over a medium-high heat. Bring to a high simmer, then reduce to a gentle simmer and cook for 20–25 minutes, or until the lentils are just tender.

Dissolve the miso thoroughly in the soup. If the miso is firm, ladle some of the soup into a small bowl with the miso, whisk until smooth, then pour it back into the donabe. Adjust the seasoning with salt, if needed.

Prepare the broccoli while the soup is cooking. Bring a saucepan of water to the boil, add the broccoli and blanch for 1–2 minutes until crisp-tender. Drain, let cool, then gently squeeze out any excess moisture. (If you have a donabe steamer, steam for 2–3 minutes instead.) Cut into 2 cm (¾ in) lengths. Toss with the ground sesame seeds and shio-koji, then drizzle with olive oil to lightly coat and toss again.

Ladle the soup into individual bowls and top each with the broccoli.

IV

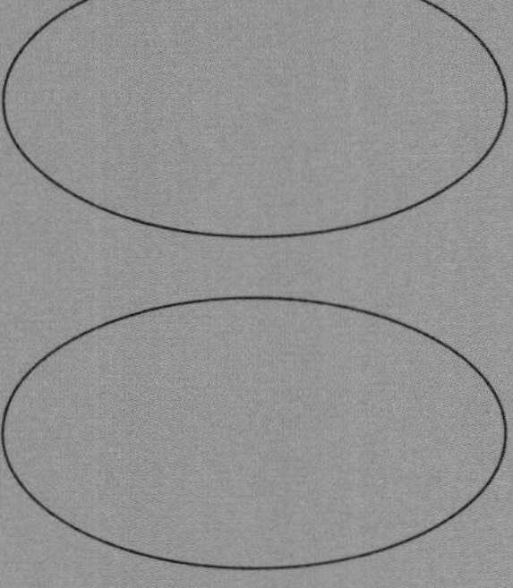

SEAFOOD

Surrounded by rich oceans in all directions, Japan has a deep-rooted seafood culture with an incredible variety of seasonal offerings. Over centuries, many preparation techniques have been refined and adapted to home cooking. I grew up eating seafood in many forms – steamed, simmered, grilled or enjoyed raw as sashimi and sushi – and I always love exploring its versatility. This chapter features simple, everyday donabe seafood dishes that let the ingredients shine, with many also perfect for gatherings. You will find some traditional flavours of Japanese home cooking and also dishes with spices or unexpected pairings for a unique touch.

Salmon Kale Saka-Mushi

SAKE-STEAMED SALMON AND KALE OVER BUTTERY SWEET POTATO

鮭とケールの酒蒸し、
さつまいものバター焼き

Serves 4

GF

For the salmon

450 g (1 lb) salmon fillet, cut into 8 or more pieces
2 tbsp Shio-Koji (page 238) or 2 tsp sea salt

For the almond butter sauce

2 tbsp almond butter
1 tbsp maple syrup
1 tbsp rice vinegar
1½ tbsp shoyu (or tamari for gluten free)

For the donabe

2 tbsp unsalted butter or extra virgin olive oil
1 satsumaimo (Japanese sweet potato) (about 400 g/14 oz), peeled and cut into 1 cm (½ in) thick rounds
1 garlic clove, coarsely minced
150 g (5½ oz) cavolo nero (Italian kale), cut widthways into 8 mm strips
Freshly ground black pepper, to taste
2 tbsp sake

To serve

Lemon wedges

This dish brings together buttery sweet potato, hearty kale and tender shio-koji-marinated salmon, layered and sake-steamed in a tagine-style donabe. The potato caramelises nicely in the donabe skillet, developing deep flavour before the kale and salmon are added. The combination of these ingredients creates magical layers of flavour, and the rich almond butter sauce brings everything together with a bold, savoury finish.

EQUIPMENT: Tagine-style donabe (or frying pan/skillet with a lid)

METHOD: Season both sides of the salmon with shio-koji and let it rest for at least 30 minutes (a few hours or overnight is better). Gently wipe off any excess marinade with a paper towel.

Whisk together the ingredients for the almond butter sauce, adding them one at a time to ensure a smooth consistency.

Heat the butter in a donabe over a medium heat. Spread the satsumaimo in a single layer and cover with a lid. Cook for 4–6 minutes, or until the bottoms are lightly golden. Flip the satsumaimo rounds and scatter the garlic in between. Evenly spread the cavolo nero on top and arrange the salmon over it. Sprinkle with black pepper and pour in the sake. Cover again and cook for about 5 minutes, or until everything is cooked through.

Uncover and squeeze some lemon juice over the top. Serve in individual bowls drizzled with the almond butter sauce.

Salmon Daikon Kasane-Ni

SALMON AND DAIKON IN GARLIC MISO BUTTER SAUCE

鮭と大根の重ね煮、
にんにく味噌バターソース

Serves 3–4

GF

For the miso sauce

4 tbsp miso
2 tbsp sake
1 tbsp mirin

For the donabe

1 tsp sea salt
450 g (1 lb) skinless salmon fillet, cut into 8-12 pieces
220 g (8 oz) daikon (mooli), cut into 2 mm thick rounds, then halved (if using a small daikon, no need to halve)
200 g (7 oz) enoki mushrooms, trimmed, halved
400 ml (14 fl oz/generous 1½ cups) Awase Dashi (page 233) or your choice of stock
1 medium carrot, julienned
2 garlic cloves, thinly sliced
1 tbsp cold unsalted butter, cut into 6-8 pieces

To serve

1 tbsp pure yuzu juice or lemon juice
coriander (cilantro) leaves
shichimi togarashi (Japanese seven-spice powder)

This dish is as easy as layering the ingredients in a donabe and pouring a quick miso sauce over the top. The salmon is partially nestled in a light dashi broth, allowing it to cook through while retaining its delicate texture and clean flavour. The butter melts into the miso-based broth, adding a deep richness, while garlic and yuzu bring bright, aromatic accents. The combination of daikon (mooli), enoki mushrooms and carrots creates a satisfying balance of textures. Make sure to slice the daikon very thin so it becomes nicely tender after the short cooking time. It's simple, comforting and perfect for an easy weeknight meal.

EQUIPMENT: Classic-style donabe (or heavy duty pot) (2.5 litre/85 fl oz)

METHOD: Whisk together the miso sauce ingredients in a small bowl and set aside.

Sprinkle salt on both sides of the salmon and let it sit for 15–30 minutes. Pat dry with a paper towel.

Arrange the daikon slices and mushrooms to cover the bottom of a donabe. Add the dashi, cover and bring to a high simmer over a medium-high heat, then reduce the heat to a low simmer and cook for 2–3 minutes.

Add the carrots and spread evenly. Place the salmon on top and pour the miso sauce over the pieces, then sprinkle the garlic over the salmon, followed by the cold butter pieces. Cover again and bring back to a simmer. Cook for 3–5 minutes, or until the salmon is cooked to your preference. Stir gently a couple of times, so the sauce will be evenly distributed.

Drizzle the yuzu juice over the salmon and garnish with coriander leaves and a sprinkle of shichimi togarashi before serving.

Asari no Yuzu-Kosho Mushi

STEAMED CLAMS AND CABBAGE IN GARLIC YUZU-KOSHO SAUCE

浅蜊の柚子胡椒蒸し

Serves 2

For the yuzu-kosho sauce

½ tsp yuzu-kosho (yuzu and green chilli pepper paste), or more to taste
½ tsp ayu (sweetfish) sauce or 1 tbsp other fish sauce
2 tbsp sake

For the donabe

generous 1 tsp sea salt
300 ml (10 fl oz/1¼ cups) water
1 garlic clove, thinly sliced
1 tbsp extra virgin olive oil
3-4 green cabbage leaves, cut into bite-size pieces
100 g (3½ oz) enoki mushrooms, trimmed and cut in half widthways
500 g (1 lb 2 oz) littleneck clams, scrubbed and cleaned (see Note)

To serve

1 tbsp pure yuzu juice or lemon juice
minced chives
ground sansho (Japanese mountain pepper)

Clams and cabbage are a classic combination I love to enjoy in spring. This dish comes together easily by layering everything into a donabe with a few simple seasonings and letting the ingredients speak for themselves. The yuzu-kosho gives a gentle aromatic kick, and a squeeze of fresh yuzu juice at the end brightens the whole dish. The clams turn plump, the cabbage becomes sweet and tender, and the broth is so flavourful that I often toss in freshly cooked pasta at the end to make a quick Japanese-style vongole – perfect for savouring every last drop.

Clams are thought to help support kidney function, ease internal heat and promote relaxation, while cabbage is said to aid digestion and strengthens the stomach. Together, they make a dish that feels both soothing and revitalising – I always feel completely relaxed after eating it.

EQUIPMENT: Classic-style donabe (or heavy duty pot) (1.2 litre/40 fl oz)

METHOD: To make the sauce, whisk together the yuzu-kosho, ayu sauce and sake in a small bowl.

Combine the garlic and olive oil in a donabe and set over a medium heat. Gently cook the garlic for about 1 minute to infuse the oil with its flavour.

Add the cabbage, mushrooms and clams. Pour in the sauce and cover with the lid. Increase the heat to medium-high and cook for 3–5 minutes, or until the clams open.

Pour in the yuzu juice, stir and serve, finished with a sprinkle of chives and ground sansho.

NOTE: To clean the clams, spread them in a shallow bowl. Dissolve the salt in the water and pour over the clams, just enough to almost cover them. Cover with a piece of kitchen foil or place in a dark, cool spot for 1–2 hours to let them purge any sand or grit. If it's warm or you plan to use them later, refrigerate the bowl and take it out 30–60 minutes before cooking. Drain, rinse and scrub the clams thoroughly. Some types of clams don't need much purging, so ask your fishmonger for advice.

Mushi-Zakana no Goma Abura Sauce

STEAMED HALIBUT WITH SIZZLING SESAME OIL SAUCE

白身魚の熱い
胡麻油ソースがけ

Serves 3–4

For the sauce

1 tbsp oyster sauce
1 tbsp shoyu (or tamari for gluten free)
½ tbsp fish sauce
1 tbsp kurozu (Japanese black vinegar)
1 tsp raw brown sugar

For the donabe

450 g (1 lb) halibut fillet, cut into 4-5 cm (2 in) cubes
1 tbsp sake
1 tsp sea salt
1 tbsp katakuriko (potato starch) (optional)
5-6 spring onions (scallions), white and green parts separated, white parts cut into fine julienne
1 garlic clove, finely sliced
60 g (2 oz) fresh root ginger, very finely julienned
1½ tbsp sesame oil
1 small carrot, finely julienned
handful of chopped fresh coriander (cilantro)

This colourful donabe dish is packed with flavour and incredibly easy to make. When hot sesame oil is drizzled over the fish, it sizzles and releases an irresistible aroma that instantly stimulates your appetite. I always love to mound a generous amount of very finely julienned spring onion (scallion) and ginger over the steamed fish. Once the sizzling oil and sauce are poured, they become so fragrant and tasty with the fish! Halibut is usually my top choice for this dish, but cod or salmon also work beautifully. The savoury sauce and bright toppings make this a satisfying main course, especially when served with rice.

EQUIPMENT: Donabe steamer (or pot with a steam basket), heatproof shallow bowl (about 21 cm/8½ in in diameter x 5 cm/2 in high)

METHOD: Stir together all the sauce ingredients in a small bowl and set aside.

Lightly sprinkle the halibut with the sake and salt. Let it sit for 15–30 minutes, then pat dry with a paper towel. If using, dust the fish lightly with katakuriko using a tea strainer.

Spread the green tops of the spring onions evenly in a heatproof shallow bowl. Arrange the halibut in an even layer on top, then scatter the garlic over the fish.

Set up the donabe steamer and bring the water to the boil. Place the bowl with the fish on the steam grate, cover and steam over a medium-high heat for 5–7 minutes, or until the fish is just cooked through.

Uncover and top the fish with the julienned white parts of the spring onions and the ginger.

Heat the sesame oil in a small pan over a medium-high heat until it starts smoking, about 1–2 minutes. Carefully drizzle the hot oil over the fish to release the aroma. The oil will sizzle, so be careful.

Sprinkle with the carrot and coriander, then pour the sauce over the fish and serve immediately. (The green spring onion tops under the fish are only for aroma and can be discarded.)

Garlic Gindara Mushi-Yaki

SIZZLING BLACK COD AND GARLIC IN OYSTER SAUCE

銀鱈とニンニクの蒸し焼き
オイスターソース風味

Serves 4

600 g (1 lb 5 oz) black cod (sablefish) fillet, cut into 5 cm (2 in) wide pieces
1 tsp sea salt
2½ tbsp oyster sauce
½ tbsp fish sauce
2 tbsp sake
2 tbsp extra virgin olive oil
8 garlic cloves, peeled and left whole
2 spring onions (scallions), cut into 2.5 cm (1 in) lengths
1 shallot, quartered
180 g (6½ oz) oyster mushrooms
1 medium carrot, thinly sliced at an angle
1 tbsp sesame oil

To serve

thinly sliced dried chilli, to garnish
chopped fresh coriander (cilantro), to garnish

Black cod, also known as sablefish, is prized for its rich, buttery texture and naturally high omega-3 content. This dish highlights its luscious flavour with a savoury marinade and a fragrant garlic-infused sauce. Everything is cooked in a donabe and finished in the oven, making it both simple and deeply flavourful. A generous amount of garlic, spring onions (scallions) and shallots caramelise beautifully as they cook, while the mushrooms and carrots soak up the bold, savoury sauce. You may be surprised how much garlic goes into the dish – and how irresistible it becomes once you taste it.

Black cod is believed to nourish blood and strengthens *qi* (vital energy). The garlic, spring onion and shallot are said to warm the body and support immunity, while carrot is believed to aid digestion and replenishes energy.

EQUIPMENT: Tagine-style donabe (or frying pan/skillet with a lid)

METHOD: Sprinkle both sides of the fish with salt and let it rest for 20–30 minutes. Pat dry well with paper towel and transfer to a resealable bag or a bowl. This process allows the fish to release excess moisture and absorb the marinade more effectively.

Stir together the oyster sauce, fish sauce and sake. Pour over the fish and let it marinate for 30 minutes.

Preheat the oven to 240°C/460°F (220°C/430°F fan).

Combine the olive oil, garlic, spring onions and shallot in a donabe. Set over a medium heat and sauté for a few minutes until aromatic. Add the fish along with the marinade, followed by the mushrooms and carrot. Drizzle with the sesame oil.

Transfer the donabe to the oven and cook for 12–15 minutes.

Sprinkle with sliced dried chilli and coriander before serving.

→ A Summer Meal: Hakko Otsumami Trio (page 42); Corn Shira-ae (page 47); Kikurage Salad (page 54); Mushi Salmon to Mame Soup (page 116); Ume Iwashi Takikomi Gohan (page 175); Matcha Madeleine (page 208)

Tai Shabu

SEA BREAM SHABU SHABU
鯛しゃぶ

Serves 4

For the dashi

- 1.2 litres (40 fl oz/5 cups) water
- 120 ml (4 fl oz/½ cup) sake
- two 5 x 10 cm (2 x 4 in) pieces kombu

For the momiji oroshi

- 200 g (7 oz) daikon (mooli), finely grated (about 4 tbsp after squeezing out excess moisture)
- 1–2 tsp kanzuri (fermented chilli and yuzu paste)

For the donabe

- 450 g (1 lb) sashimi-grade sea bream fillet, skin on
- 6 medium napa cabbage leaves, cut into bite-size pieces
- 150 g (5½ oz) oyster mushrooms
- 1 carrot, shaved into strips with a peeler
- 180 g (6½ oz) rehydrated wakame, cut into bite-size pieces
- 4 spring onions (scallions), cut thinly at a long angle
- 400 g (14 oz) soft tofu, cut into 8–9 pieces
- Kaeshi Ponzu (page 239), to serve

Tai (sea bream) is a cherished fish in Japan, especially in spring when it's at its peak flavour. I enjoy it as sashimi, sushi or crudo, but tai shabu – thinly sliced sea bream swished lightly in hot broth – has a special place in my heart. The simple broth lets the fish's delicate sweetness shine, and everyone can cook their own slices at the table. Dipping the fish in ponzu and topping it with refreshing momiji oroshi (grated daikon with chilli paste) makes it even more memorable. I also love saving some broth to finish with a simple shime (finishing course) of somen noodles (page 21).

Sea bream provides easy-to-digest nourishment and is thought to refresh energy and calm the mind. Napa cabbage, wakame, tofu and momiji oroshi are said to aid digestion, circulation and hydration. This dish may support digestive health, fluid balance and emotional stability.

EQUIPMENT: Classic-style donabe (or heavy duty pot) (2.5 litre/85 fl oz)

METHOD: To prepare the dashi, combine the water, sake and kombu in a donabe and soak for 30 minutes.

To prepare the momiji oroshi, mix the daikon with the kanzuri in a small bowl.

Wrap each fish fillet in a paper towel and place on a strainer, skin-side up. Bring a saucepan of water to the boil and pour over the fish to lightly cook the skin. Remove the paper towel and immediately transfer the fillets to a bowl of iced water.

Pat the fillets dry with paper towel, cut into thin slices and arrange on a serving platter, skin-side up. Arrange the napa cabbage, mushrooms, carrot, wakame, spring onions and tofu on another serving platter.

Set the donabe on a table-top stove, and bring to a simmer over a medium-heat. Remove the kombu. Increase the heat to medium-high, then add some napa cabbage, mushrooms and tofu, and cook for 2–3 minutes.

Add some spring onions, carrot and wakame, then swish a slice of fish in the hot broth until just cooked (I like it rare and wrap some spring onions inside). Dip in the ponzu and enjoy with the momiji oroshi. Pick and dip any other ingredients as they are cooked with or without momiji oroshi, too. Continue cooking and enjoying the ingredients until finished.

NOTE: If you can source salt-pickled cherry blossom leaves, arrange the fillets on quickly rinsed leaves about 30 minutes before serving, to infuse a delicate aroma. You can also soak and rinse salt-pickled cherry blossom flowers and add them to the shabu shabu or shime (as shown in page 23) course for a seasonal accent.

Salmon Asari Miso Tomato Stew

SALMON AND CLAM STEW WITH MISO TOMATO SAUCE

鮭と浅蜊の味噌トマトシチュー

Serves 3–4

For the miso tomato sauce

- 2 tbsp miso
- 2 tbsp tomato paste
- 1 tsp kanzuri (fermented chilli and yuzu paste), or more to taste (optional)
- 60 ml (2 fl oz/¼ cup) sake
- 120 ml (4 fl oz/½ cup) Awase Dashi (page 233) or your choice of stock

For the donabe

- 450 g (1 lb) salmon fillet, cut into 6-8 pieces
- ½ tsp sea salt, or more to taste
- 1 tbsp extra virgin olive oil, plus extra to serve (optional)
- 1 shallot, halved lengthways, then thinly sliced widthways
- 2 garlic cloves, thinly sliced
- 150 g (5½ oz) oyster mushrooms, trimmed, cut into bite-size pieces if needed
- 6-8 littleneck clams, scrubbed and cleaned
- 1 small carrot, thinly cut at an angle
- freshly ground black pepper, to taste

To serve

- chopped dill or your choice of herb
- kurozu (Japanese black vinegar) (optional)

This quick donabe dish pairs rich salmon with a bold, aromatic sauce made from miso, tomato paste and sake. A touch of kanzuri (fermented chilli and yuzu paste) adds gentle spice, but you can leave it out for a milder taste. The sauce is incredibly versatile – it works beautifully with other proteins or even as a base for vegetables. I prefer using a thick-body donabe for this dish, as it retains heat exceptionally well and allows the ingredients to cook gently in their own moisture, resulting in deep, concentrated flavours.

Salmon is believed to nourish stamina and gently refresh the body. Miso and garlic are thought to strengthen digestion, circulation and immune function, while tomato paste is said to help cool mild internal heat. This dish may support energy renewal, digestive health and a balanced, light feeling.

EQUIPMENT: Classic-style donabe (or heavy duty pot) (1.8 litre/60 fl oz)

METHOD: Whisk together the miso tomato sauce ingredients in a bowl and set aside.

Season both sides of the salmon with salt and let it rest for 30 minutes. Pat dry with a paper towel.

Heat the olive oil in a donabe over a medium heat. Add the shallot and garlic and sauté until aromatic, about 1 minute. Add the mushrooms and sauté for another 2–3 minutes. Pour in the sauce, cover with a lid and bring to a simmer.

Add the clams, salmon and carrot, cover again and cook for about 5 minutes, or until the clams open and everything is cooked through.

Season with black pepper and adjust the seasoning with additional salt, if needed.

Serve in individual bowls, garnished with dill and splashed with extra olive oil and kurozu, if desired.

Gyokai no Saka-Mushi

SAKE-STEAMED SEAFOOD AND VEGETABLES WITH GARLIC SAKE-KASU SAUCE

魚介と野菜の酒蒸し

Serves 4

For the garlic sake-kasu sauce

- 2 garlic cloves, finely grated
- ½ tsp Dijon mustard
- 1 tbsp Shio-Koji (page 238), or more to taste
- 2 tsp lemon juice
- 1 tbsp sake-kasu (sake lees)
- 2 tbsp extra virgin olive oil
- 4–6 tbsp coconut yoghurt or Greek-style yoghurt

For the donabe

- 350 g (12 oz) Chilean sea bass fillet, cut into 8 pieces
- 180 g (6½ oz) medium prawns (shrimp), peeled and deveined
- 1–1½ tsp herb salt
- 2 tbsp extra virgin olive oil, or more to taste
- 1 shallot, thinly sliced widthways
- 4 shiitake mushrooms, trimmed, thinly sliced
- 2 baby (bell) peppers, cut into thin strips
- 1 small carrot, thinly cut at an angle
- 120 g (4 oz) asparagus, woody ends trimmed, cut into thirds at an angle
- 60 ml (2 fl oz/¼ cup) sake
- freshly ground black pepper, to taste
- dill leaves, to garnish

This dish was inspired by my trip to Biarritz, a beautiful coastal town in the Basque region of France. I enjoyed simply prepared seafood with just a touch of seasoning and olive oil. I like using my tagine-style donabe for a similar preparation, steaming white sea bass and vegetables together with a hint of herb salt. You can use a kind of herb salt you like, or simple sea salt can also work well. The sake-kasu garlic sauce is like my version of aioli and it's quite garlicky – rich in probiotic and has more complex umami flavours.

For the fish, besides Chilean sea bass, other higher oil content fish such as halibut, black cod or salmon work well as an alternative.

EQUIPMENT: Tagine-style donabe (or frying pan/skillet with a lid)

METHOD: To make the sauce, whisk together the garlic, mustard, shio-koji, lemon juice and sake-kasu in a bowl. Slowly whisk in the olive oil to emulsify. Add the yoghurt and whisk until smooth. Taste and adjust the seasoning with more shio-koji, if needed.

Season both sides of the fish and prawns with the herb salt and let rest for 20–30 minutes. Pat dry with paper towels.

Heat the olive oil in a donabe over a medium-high heat. Add the shallot, mushrooms, peppers and carrot, and stir. Cover with the lid and cook for a couple of minutes, stirring once or twice.

Add the fish, prawns and asparagus, then pour in the sake and cover again. Cook for 4–5 minutes, or until everything is cooked through. Season with black pepper and sprinkle with a generous amount of dill.

Serve in individual bowls, drizzled with more olive oil. Enjoy with the sauce on the side.

NOTE: The sauce is also great with steamed fish, crab cakes, crudités or vegetables, and can be easily adapted to different dishes. White sea bass is a mild, meaty fish, but other firm white fish, such as halibut, striped bass, grouper or mahi mahi, also work beautifully, as well as black cod or salmon.

Suzuki no Nitsuke

SOY-SIMMERED EUROPEAN SEA BASS

鱸の煮付け

Serves 2

- fillets (about 180 g/6½ oz each) European sea bass (branzino) or your choice of fish, cut into pieces as needed
- tsp sea salt, or to taste
- 60 g (2 oz) mangetout (snow peas), trimmed and side string removed
- one 5 x 10 cm (2 x 4 in) piece kombu
- 180 ml (6 fl oz/¾ cup) water
- 90 ml (3 fl oz/6 tbsp) sake
- tbsp shoyu (or tamari for gluten free)
- tbsp Okinawa black sugar or raw brown sugar
- tbsp mirin
- knob (about 20 g/¾ oz) fresh root ginger, very finely julienned
- 120 g (4 oz) king oyster mushrooms, cut into bite-size slices
- ground sansho (Japanese mountain pepper), to serve

European sea bass (branzino), called *suzuki* in Japanese, is a delicate, mild fish that works beautifully in nitsuke, a classic Japanese technique for gently simmering fish in a savoury-sweet soy-based broth. I grew up eating seasonal fish nitsuke made by my mom, and my favourite was fillet of komochi karei (roe-bearing flounder), but it's not something I can find at regular markets here in LA. Still, I love making nitsuke with fresh branzino fillets, which absorb the flavours beautifully. The lightly sweet and savoury sauce brings out the natural umami of the fish without overpowering it. This dish is quick to make yet deeply comforting.

EQUIPMENT: Classic-style donabe (or heavy duty pot) (1.8 litre/60 fl oz)

METHOD: Sprinkle both sides of the fish with salt and let it rest for 20–30 minutes. Pat dry with paper towel.

Bring a saucepan of water to the boil and blanch the mangetout for 30 seconds. Drain and immediately transfer to a bowl of iced water to retain their bright colour. Drain again and pat dry with paper towel.

Combine the kombu, water, sake, shoyu, sugar and mirin in a donabe and let the kombu soak for 15 minutes or longer.

Set the donabe over a medium heat and bring to a simmer. Gently place the fish fillets into the broth in a single layer, then add the ginger and mushrooms. Place a drop lid or baking parchment cartouche directly on the surface of the ingredients to help the flavours be absorbed evenly. Cover, bring back to a simmer and cook for 5–6 minutes.

Add the mangetout and turn off the heat. Serve in individual bowls and finish with a sprinkle of ground sansho.

FLAVOUR VARIATION: You can also try this with other types of fish, such as sea bream (snapper), mahi mahi, or salmon – something not too fatty works best.

Kani Kabocha Tofu Gratin

CRAB AND KABOCHA GRATIN WITH TOFU CREAM SAUCE

蟹と南瓜の
豆腐クリームグラタン

Serves 4

For the tofu cream

300 g (10½ oz) medium-firm tofu
60 ml (2 fl oz/¼ cup) pure soya milk
½ tbsp kudzu starch
2 tbsp Saikyo miso or other sweet white miso
1 tbsp extra virgin olive oil
½ tsp sea salt

For the donabe

2 tbsp extra virgin olive oil
250 g (9 oz) kabocha squash, skin thinly peeled, cut into 2 cm (¾ in) cubes
150 g (5½ oz) shimeji mushrooms, trimmed
2 garlic cloves, thinly sliced
1 tsp fennel seeds
2 tbsp sake
2 tbsp water
½ tbsp Shio-Koji (page 238), or more to taste
freshly ground black pepper, to taste
220 g (8 oz) crab meat
50 g (1¾ oz) Gruyère cheese, grated, or more to taste

To serve

lemon zest
chopped dill

This hearty oven-baked donabe dish is one of my favourite things to make in the winter. The sweet kabocha squash, shimeji mushrooms and tender crab meat pair so well with the creamy tofu sauce – rich and full of flavour but still light. I love pulling it out of the oven when the surface is golden and bubbling – it's so warm and irresistible.

EQUIPMENT: Classic-style donabe (or heavy duty pot) (1.2 litre/40 fl oz)

METHOD: Preheat the oven to 240°C/460°F (220°C/430°F fan).

To make the tofu cream, place the tofu in a shallow tray and top with a flat tray or small cutting board. Add a weight 1–1.5 times the tofu's weight and let it sit for 30 minutes to remove excess moisture. Drain the liquid and pat the tofu dry with a paper towel.

Whisk the soya milk and kudzu starch in a small bowl until smooth. Combine the tofu, miso, olive oil, salt and the soya milk mixture in a food processor. Process until very smooth.

Heat the olive oil in a donabe over medium heat. Add the kabocha and mushrooms and sauté for about 2 minutes until the mushrooms are soft. Add the garlic and fennel seeds, and sauté another 2 minutes. Add the sake and water, cover and cook for about 5 minutes, or until the liquid is mostly reduced. Add the shio-koji and some black pepper and stir. Turn off the heat.

Top with the crab meat and spread the tofu cream, followed by the cheese, evenly in layers over the top. Bake in the oven, uncovered, for 20–25 minutes until the surface is golden brown and bubbling.

Mix the lemon zest and dill and sprinkle over the top to serve.

FLAVOUR VARIATION: The tofu cream sauce is versatile – you can add meat or keep it completely plant-based by omitting the crab and using plant-based cheese. Some of my other favourite combinations are sautéed spinach and chicken, or corn and short pasta.

Mushi Salmon to Mame Soup

STEAMED BLACK GARLIC SALMON AND CLAMS WITH PEA SOUP

蒸した鮭とえんどう豆のスープ

Serves 3–4

For the steamed salmon

1 small orange, cut into thin round slices
450 g (1 lb) salmon, cut into 8 or more pieces
4 or more black garlic cloves, sliced in half (optional)
8 littleneck clams, scrubbed and cleaned (page 101)

For the pea soup

2 tbsp extra virgin olive oil
1 shallot, minced
2 garlic cloves, thinly sliced
1 small carrot, thinly sliced
150 g (5½ oz) shimeji mushrooms, trimmed
1 bay leaf
60 ml (2 fl oz/¼ cup) sake
1 litre (34 fl oz/4¼ cups) Shojin Dashi (page 233) or vegetable stock
120 ml (4 fl oz/½ cup) Saikyo miso or other sweet white miso
150 g (5½ oz) garden peas
200 g (7 oz) asparagus, woody ends trimmed; stalks cut into 8 mm rounds, tips kept whole
sea salt, to taste

To serve

Kaeshi Ponzu (page 239)
freshly ground black pepper
thinly sliced basil
lemon zest

What I love about using a donabe steamer is that you can do steaming and simmering separately in one donabe at the same time. As the soup simmers in the bottom, the salmon and clams gently steam above, becoming lightly infused with the delicate aromas of the orange. The black garlic, although it's optional, adds a mellow sweetness, and a drizzle of ponzu at the end brings everything together with a bright, savoury touch. I also like to finish the soup with a sprinkle of sliced basil (chopped dill is also good) and lemon zest that adds a refreshing lift. If you don't have a donabe steamer for the double tasks, you can prepare the soup in a classic-style donabe (or heavy duty pot) and steam the fish separately.

EQUIPMENT: Donabe steamer (or pot with a steam basket)

METHOD: To prepare the steamed salmon, spread the orange slices evenly on the steam grate of a donabe steamer. Arrange the salmon on top, and place a clove of black garlic (if using) on each piece of salmon. Nestle the clams around the salmon.

For the soup, heat the olive oil in the donabe over a medium heat and add the shallot and garlic. Sauté for about 1 minute. Add the carrot and mushrooms, and sauté for another 2 minutes. Add the bay leaf, deglaze with the sake, then add the dashi and bring to a simmer. Stir in the miso until fully dissolved. If the miso is firm, ladle some of the soup into a small bowl with the miso, whisk until smooth, then pour it back into the donabe.

Add the peas and asparagus, then adjust the seasoning with salt, if needed. Bring back to a simmer. Set the steam grate with the salmon (over the soup) on the donabe and cover with the lid. Cook for 4–5 minutes, or until the salmon is cooked and clams have opened.

Uncover and carefully transfer the steam grate with the seafood to nestle in the flipped lid. Divide the salmon and clams among bowls and enjoy with a drizzle of ponzu. For the soup, season with black pepper and mix in the basil, then divide among separate bowls and sprinkle with lemon zest, to taste.

FLAVOUR VARIATIONS: You can use different ingredients in the soup, such as diced kabu (Japanese turnip), okra, potatoes or frozen artichoke hearts. Artichoke pairs beautifully with peas and brings extra health benefits.

For a vegan version, replace the salmon and black garlic with large cubes of medium-firm tofu. Steam the tofu over the soup and serve with the ponzu, or gently place the tofu on top of the soup when serving.

Ishikari Nabe

MISO BUTTER HOTPOT WITH SALMON AND SCALLOPS

石狩鍋

Serves 4–5

VG OP

GF

For the miso base

- 3 tbsp miso
- 2 tbsp Saikyo miso or other sweet white miso
- 60 ml (2 fl oz/¼ cup) sake
- 2 tbsp mirin
- 1 tbsp shoyu (or tamari for gluten free)

For the donabe

- 200 g (7 oz) shirataki (konnyaku) noodles, rinsed and drained
- 1 litre (34 fl oz/4¼ cups) Awase Dashi (page 233) or your choice of stock
- 7–8 medium napa cabbage leaves, cut into bite-size pieces
- 200 g (7 oz) enoki mushrooms, trimmed
- 300 g (10½ oz) satsumaimo (Japanese sweet potato), peeled and cut into 6 mm (¼ in) thick rounds
- 350 g (12 oz) salmon fillet, cut into 4 cm (1½ in) pieces
- 250 g (9 oz) scallops
- 150 g (5½ oz) chrysanthemum leaves (or other leafy greens of choice), cut into 5 cm (2 in) pieces
- 2 tbsp unsalted butter, cut into slices

To serve

- 50 g (1¾ oz) ikura (salmon roe)
- shichimi togarashi (Japanese seven spice powder)

Ishikari nabe is Ishikari nabe a traditional hotpot from Hokkaido, featuring salmon and potatoes simmered in a savoury miso-based broth. I like to keep my version simple, focusing on quality ingredients and finishing with a couple of slices of butter to enrich the broth with an irresistible aroma. For shime (finishing course), the rich broth is perfect for making ojiya (quick porridge) with a pour of beaten egg, or you can enjoy it as classic Hokkaido-style miso ramen topped with corn.

EQUIPMENT: Classic-style donabe (or heavy duty pot) (2.5 litre/85 fl oz)

METHOD: Whisk together the miso base ingredients in a small bowl until smooth.

Bring a saucepan of water to the boil, add the shirataki noodles and boil for 2 minutes (see Note). Drain and cut into shorter lengths if needed.

Set the donabe on a table-top stove. Add the dashi and bring to a simmer over a medium-high heat. Add the cabbage, mushrooms, satsumaimo and noodles. Cover and bring back to a simmer, then cook for 3–5 minutes, or until everything is heated through and the cabbage is soft.

Stir in the miso base and bring back to a simmer. Add the salmon and scallops, and cook until just cooked through, about 2–3 minutes.

Add the chrysanthemum leaves and butter. Turn off the heat and let the leaves wilt and the butter melt into the broth.

Serve in individual bowls, topped with ikura, with shichimi togarashi on the side.

NOTE: Blanching the shirataki noodles helps remove its earthy aroma, so it won't affect the broth flavour.

FLAVOUR VARIATION: The broth is versatile – you can add sliced pork belly with the seafood for a heartier version, or make it plant-based with Shojin Dashi (page 233), tofu and a variety of mushrooms (and omit the butter).

Ebi Shiitake Shumai

STEAMED PRAWN-STUFFED SHIITAKE MUSHROOMS
海老の椎茸焼売

Serves 4

8–10 shiitake mushrooms, caps and stalks separated (very hard end trimmed)
250 g (9 oz) peeled and deveined prawns (shrimp), rinsed and patted dry
½ tbsp sake
1 tsp sea salt
1 tbsp mayonnaise
1 tsp sesame oil
½ shallot, finely minced (about 2 tbsp)
2 tsp katakuriko (potato starch), plus more for dusting
napa cabbage leaves, for steaming (optional)

For the sizzling sauce

1 spring onion (scallion), finely minced (about 1–1½ tbsp)
1 tsp raw brown sugar
½ tbsp finely grated fresh root ginger
1 garlic clove, finely grated
1 tsp sliced dried chilli
2 tbsp sesame oil
1 tbsp sake
2 tbsp shoyu (or tamari for gluten free)
1 tbsp pure yuzu juice or lemon juice

These dim sum-style steamed stuffed mushrooms are simple to prepare and quite irresistible. In Japan, shiitake stems are highly valued for their depth of flavour, so instead of discarding them, I blend them into the prawn (shrimp) filling after trimming only the very hard tip. Steamed in a donabe, the prawns and meaty shiitake come together into juicy, tender bites, finished with a sizzling aromatic sauce that adds savoury depth and a touch of heat.

EQUIPMENT: Donabe steamer (or pot with a steam basket)

METHOD: Combine the shiitake stalks, prawns, sake, salt, mayonnaise and sesame oil in a food processor. Pulse 8–10 times, or until well blended but the prawns are still slightly chunky for texture. Transfer to a bowl.

Combine the shallot and katakuriko in a small bowl and toss well. Add to the prawn mixture and mix with a spatula until well combined.

Lightly dust the inner side of each shiitake cap with katakuriko. Divide the filling into 8–10 pieces and stuff each cap with the filling, smoothing the surface.

For the sauce, combine the spring onion, sugar, ginger, garlic and chilli in a bowl. Heat the sesame oil in a small pan over a medium-high heat until it starts smoking, about 1–2 minutes. Carefully drizzle the hot oil into the onion mixture. The oil will sizzle, so be careful. Immediately add the sake to the same pan (it will sizzle again) and let it briefly cook off the alcohol, or bring it to the boil separately over a medium heat. Pour into the mixture, followed by the shoyu and yuzu juice. Stir well.

Set up the donabe steamer and bring the water to the boil. If desired, line the steam grate with napa cabbage leaves and let them wilt slightly before adding the mushrooms. Arrange the stuffed mushrooms in a single layer, cover and steam over a medium-high heat for 5–7 minutes, or until cooked through.

Serve immediately with the sizzling sauce on the side.

NOTE: Yield and cooking time may vary depending on the size of the mushrooms. If a piece is on the larger side, you can cut it into bite-size portions when serving.

FLAVOUR VARIATIONS: Blend some scallop into the filling for extra sweetness.

The stuffed shiitake are also delicious served with a small dab of yuzu-kosho (yuzu and green chilli pepper paste) on the side.

Gindara Yuba Nabe

BLACK COD AND TOFU SKIN HOTPOT

銀鱈と湯葉の煮込み鍋

Serves 4

For the soup base

2 tbsp miso
3 tbsp shoyu (or tamari for gluten free)
60 ml (2 fl oz/¼ cup) sake
1 tsp tobanjan (Chinese chilli bean paste)
1 tsp raw brown sugar
480 ml (17 fl oz/2 cups) Tori Dashi (page 236), or your choice of stock

For the donabe

600 g (1 lb 5 oz) black cod (sablefish) fillet, cut into 5 cm (2 in) wide pieces
1 tsp sea salt
katakuriko (potato starch), for dusting
150 g (5½ oz) soybean sprouts
150 g (5½ oz) soft yuba (tofu skin), cut into bite-size pieces
2 garlic cloves, thinly sliced
½ tbsp minced fresh root ginger
200 g (7 oz) enoki mushrooms, trimmed
2 baby pak choi (bok choi), cut into bite-size pieces

To serve

1 tbsp toasted white sesame seeds
1 tbsp toasted pine nuts
½ tsp sliced dried chilli
minced spring onion (scallion)
toasted sesame oil

Black cod (sablefish) has a buttery texture and rich flavour that stand out beautifully in donabe hotpots. In this dish, it's simmered with soft yuba (tofu skin) in a Chinese-style broth full of warming aromatics, creating a delicate yet satisfying combination. As the ingredients simmer, the broth develops even more layers of flavour. You can also make it with other fish, such as salmon or halibut. For shime (finishing course), I often add extra dashi to the remaining broth and cook ramen noodles directly in the donabe to enjoy every last drop.

Black cod and yuba are believed to help nourish the body, replenish moisture and support energy. Warming aromatics like garlic and ginger are said to stimulate digestion and circulation, while toasted nuts and fresh herbs gently strengthen resilience and clear internal heat. This dish may be good for recovery from fatigue and restoring healthy balance.

EQUIPMENT: Classic-style donabe (or heavy duty pot) (2.5 litre/85 fl oz)

METHOD: To make the soup base, whisk together the miso, shoyu, sake, tobanjan and sugar in a bowl, then whisk in the dashi until smooth.

Sprinkle both sides of the fish with salt and let it rest for 20–30 minutes. Pat dry with paper towel and dust both sides with katakuriko right before cooking.

Pile the soybean sprouts, yuba, garlic, ginger and mushrooms into a donabe. Pour in the soup base, cover and bring to a high simmer over a medium-high heat. Add the fish and the stems of the pak choi to the donabe. Reduce the heat to a simmer, and continue to cook for 4–5 minutes until everything is cooked through. Add the top parts of the pak choi and let them wilt.

Mix the sesame seeds, pine nuts and chilli in a small bowl. Sprinkle over the donabe just before serving. Sprinkle with spring onion and drizzle with sesame oil to finish.

NOTES: Dusting the fish with katakuriko seals in moisture, keeps the texture tender and gently thickens the broth while adding a soft coating to the surface.

FLAVOUR VARIATION: Instead of soft yuba, cubed soft tofu works well in this dish, too.

Kaki no Dote Nabe

OYSTER HOTPOT WITH MISO-RIMMED BROTH

牡蠣の土手鍋

Serves 1–2

For the dote miso

- 100 g (3½ oz) miso (a combination of hatcho miso and white miso in the ratio of 2:1 to 1:1)
- 1 tbsp sake, or more to taste
- 1 garlic clove, finely grated
- 1 tsp finely grated fresh root ginger

For the donabe

- 250 g (9 oz) shucked oysters
- 1 tsp sea salt
- 1 tbsp katakuriko (potato starch)
- 2–3 medium napa cabbage leaves, cut into bite-size pieces
- 100 g (3½ oz) enoki mushrooms, trimmed
- 100 g (3½ oz) medium-firm tofu, cut into quarters
- 2 spring onions (scallions), thinly cut at an angle into 4 cm (1½ in) lengths
- 300–400 ml (10–14 fl oz/1¼–1½ cups) Awase Dashi (page 233) or your choice of stock
- 50 g (1¾ oz) seri (Japanese water dropwort) or other leafy greens, such as watercress, cut into 4 cm (1½ in) lengths

This traditional hotpot from Hiroshima, a region famous for its oysters, is something I love to whip up quickly just for myself – and it's always so satisfying. *Dote* (土手) means 'embankment', and the dish gets its name from the way miso is spread along the rim of the donabe to form a 'bank' before adding the broth and ingredients. As the donabe heats, the miso bakes and releases a wonderful aroma, and you gradually dissolve it into the broth as you cook and eat, adjusting the flavour to your liking. For shime (finishing course), I like adding extra dashi and par-cooked udon to soak up the rich broth.

Oysters are thought to be especially good for nourishing the blood and easing dryness, fatigue, internal heat and emotional restlessness. Simmered with miso and warming aromatics, they create a dish that gently restores both body and mind – it's no wonder they're called the 'milk of the ocean' in Japan.

EQUIPMENT: Classic-style donabe (or heavy duty pot) (800 ml/27 fl oz)

METHOD: To make the dote miso, whisk together the miso, sake, garlic and ginger in a bowl until it becomes a smooth paste. Add more sake if the paste is too thick.

To clean the oysters, combine them with the salt and katakuriko in a bowl and mix quickly by hand. Drain, rinse thoroughly with cold water, then drain well. Keep chilled.

Spread the dote miso along the upper sides of the donabe up to the rim, leaving the bottom uncovered. Spread the napa cabbage in the bottom and arrange the enoki mushrooms, tofu and spring onions on top.

Set the donabe on a table-top stove. Pour in about 200 ml (7 fl oz/scant 1 cup) dashi, cover and set over a medium heat. Bring to a simmer. Add more dashi, if needed, then add the seri and oysters. Cover again and bring back to a simmer. Cook for a few minutes until the oysters are cooked through. The dote miso will begin to dissolve during cooking.

To serve at the table, gently dissolve some of the remaining dote miso into the broth with chopsticks, then scoop the broth and ingredients into individual bowls. The broth will be quite rich and salty, so it can be enjoyed more like a sauce.

FLAVOUR VARIATIONS: Instead of hatcho miso and white miso, you can also use red and white misos, or just a single kind of miso. The flavour is very flexible.

You can also make this with other proteins, such as prawns (shrimp), chicken or pork belly, instead of oysters. For a plant-based version, I like sliced yamaimo (Japanese mountain yam) with a vegan dashi, which adds a rich texture to the broth.

V

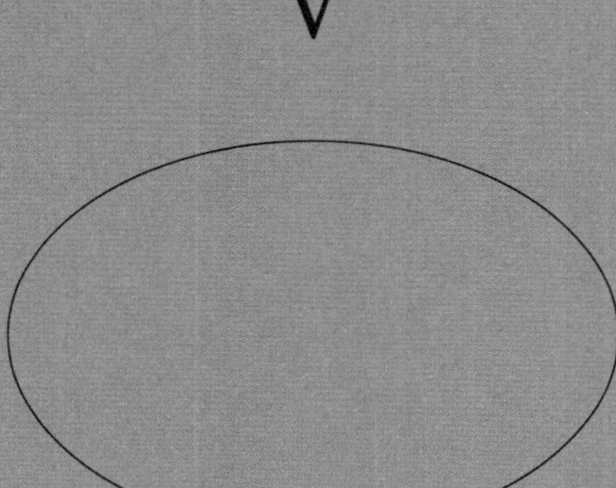

MEAT

Meat is the highlight in this chapter, but the dishes are prepared with a variety of vegetables and other plant-based ingredients for a wholesome, balanced meal. I enjoy meat in moderation as part of a holistic approach to everyday cooking. The dishes in this chapter are made with ingredients I have easy access to – chicken, pork and beef – but you can adapt them as you like. Lamb also works beautifully in many of them. For recipes that call for very thinly sliced meat, you can usually find pre-sliced cuts at a Japanese or Asian grocery store, or ask your trusted butcher to slice them for you. These are the kinds of dishes that bring people to the table again and again.

Kei-Chan

SIZZLING SHOYU CHICKEN AND CABBAGE
鶏ちゃん

Serves 4

For the marinade

1 garlic clove, finely grated
1 tbsp finely grated fresh root ginger
1 tsp tobanjan (Chinese chilli bean paste) (optional)
1 tbsp miso (aged brown rice or red miso is preferred)
2½ tbsp shoyu (or tamari for gluten free)
1½ tbsp mirin
1 tsp sesame oil

For the donabe

450 g (1 lb) skinless, boneless chicken thighs, cut into bite-size pieces
1 tbsp sesame oil
5–6 medium green cabbage leaves, cut into bite-size pieces
150 g (5½ oz) shimeji mushrooms, trimmed
1 medium carrot, julienned
100 g (3½ oz) garlic chives, cut into 5 cm (2 in) lengths
sliced dried chilli, to serve (optional)

Kei-chan is a beloved (and humble) local dish from Gifu, Japan. During my visits there, I was so drawn to this homely chicken stir-fry that's found everywhere, from izakaya and restaurants to food courts at motorway rest stops. It's usually made with chicken and cabbage in either a miso- or soy-based marinade, and cooked until sizzling. It's so popular that you can even find a wide variety of pre-made seasoning pastes for Kei-chan at local grocery stores! I especially love the soy-based version, so I came up with my own donabe-style version, also much less sweet than what I tasted in Gifu – and it's so delicious. This dish is especially nice served over freshly cooked rice to make a hearty donburi-style meal.

It is thought that chicken supports energy and stamina, while cabbage helps soothe digestion and gently detoxify the body. Ginger and garlic are said to boost blood circulation and immune strength. This dish may be helpful when you're feeling tired or need a warm, invigorating meal.

EQUIPMENT: Tagine-style donabe (or frying pan/skillet with a lid)

METHOD: Whisk together all the ingredients for the marinade in a bowl. Add the chicken and mix well. Let marinate in the refrigerator for at least 30 minutes.

Spread the sesame oil across the bottom of a donabe. Arrange the cabbage evenly over the base, then arrange the marinated chicken over the cabbage. Top with the mushrooms and carrot. Cover with the lid and set over a medium heat. When it begins to sizzle, about 2–3 minutes, continue to cook for 10–15 minutes, or until the chicken is cooked through, stirring a few times during cooking to ensure even doneness.

Add the garlic chives, cover again and cook for another minute, just until wilted. Add the dried chilli, if using, and stir once more before serving.

NOTE: A tagine-style donabe with a sturdy, flat bottom is perfect for this recipe – it heats evenly to the core and retains heat beautifully. You can also use another wide-bottomed donabe that's dry-heat safe, or a regular frying pan (skillet).

FLAVOUR VARIATION: I often enjoy the dish with a good squeeze of lemon when served. It adds a nice fresh touch to the hearty dish.

Teba Daikon Nabe

CHICKEN WING AND DAIKON HOTPOT

手羽大根鍋

Serves 4

For the broth

- one 5 x 5 cm (2 x 2 in) piece kombu
- 850 ml (29 fl oz/generous 3½ cups) Tori Dashi (page 236) or your choice of stock

For the donabe

- 600 g (1 lb 5 oz) chicken wings, drumettes and midsections separated
- 1 tsp sea salt, plus more for the broth, to taste
- 2 tbsp katakuriko (potato starch)
- 1 tbsp extra virgin olive oil
- 250 g (9 oz) daikon (mooli), cut into oblique slices
- 1 tbsp finely julienned fresh root ginger
- 80 ml (2½ fl oz/⅓ cup) sake
- 1 tbsp shiro shoyu (or 1 tsp sea salt for gluten free)
- 50 g (1¾ oz) mung bean glass noodles, cut shorter if needed
- 150 g (5½ oz) enoki mushrooms, trimmed
- 4-5 spring onions (scallions), thinly cut at an angle
- freshly ground black pepper, to taste

To serve

- toasted sesame oil
- sliced dried chilli
- kanzuri (fermented chilli and yuzu paste)

Chicken wings and daikon (mooli) are a classic pairing in Japanese cooking, and this hotpot is my favourite way to enjoy them – it always makes me feel so warm inside. Pan-frying the chicken and daikon before simmering adds depth to the soothing broth, just lightly seasoned with shiro shoyu. When done, the chicken becomes incredibly juicy – you can pull the meat off the bones with ease (or more accurately, you can pull the bones off the meat with your fingers) and the daikon turns meltingly tender. I love adding glass noodles and mushrooms at the end to soak up all the goodness and turn it into a complete one-pot meal.

EQUIPMENT: Classic-style donabe (or heavy duty pot) (2.5 litre/85 fl oz)

METHOD: To prepare the broth, combine the kombu and dashi in a donabe and let soak for at least 30 minutes.

Season the chicken wings with 1 teaspoon sea salt and let them marinate for at least 30 minutes, or up to overnight. I often use a resealable bag for convenience. Dust the chicken wings evenly with katakuriko just before starting to cook.

Bring the broth to a gentle simmer over a medium heat, then remove the kombu. Keep the broth hot over a low heat, making sure it doesn't reduce.

Meanwhile, heat the olive oil in a sauté pan over a medium-high heat. Add the chicken wings and sear for about 1–2 minutes per side until lightly golden. Transfer to the donabe.

In the same pan (no need to wipe it clean), sear the daikon slices for 1–2 minutes per side, until lightly golden. They don't need to be cooked through. Transfer to the donabe.

Add the ginger and sake to the donabe, cover with the lid and bring to a high simmer over a medium-high heat. Reduce to a gentle simmer and cook for 15 minutes.

Add the shiro shoyu, glass noodles, mushrooms and spring onions. Cover and simmer for another 5 minutes. Adjust the seasoning with sea salt and black pepper, if needed.

Finish with a splash of sesame oil and a sprinkle of dried chilli.

Serve in individual bowls and enjoy with a dab of kanzuri or your preferred condiment.

NOTE: Dusting the chicken wings with katakuriko (potato starch) helps seal in the flavour and moisture. You can also use arrowroot or plain (all-purpose) flour, if preferred.

Tōnyu Tan Tan Nabe

PORK AND VEGETABLES IN SOYA MILK AND SESAME MISO BROTH
豆乳担々鍋

Serves 2–3

For the seasoned pork

1 tbsp sesame oil
1 garlic clove, minced
½ tbsp minced fresh root ginger
220 g (8 oz) minced (ground) pork
2 tsp tobanjan (Chinese chilli bean paste)
2 tbsp sake
1 tbsp oyster sauce
freshly ground black pepper, to taste

For the tan tan broth

2 tbsp miso
2 tbsp white sesame paste (tahini can work too)
180 ml (6 fl oz/¾ cup) Tori Dashi (page 236) or your choice of stock
420 ml (14½ fl oz/generous 1¾ cups) pure soya milk
sea salt, to taste (optional)

For the donabe

50 g (1¾ oz) shimeji mushrooms, trimmed
200 g (7 oz) medium-firm tofu, cut into 8–9 pieces
100 g (3½ oz) enoki mushrooms, trimmed and halved
150 g (5½ oz) bean sprouts
1–2 baby pak choi (bok choi), cut into bite-size pieces

To serve

ground toasted white sesame seeds
minced spring onion (scallion)
la-yu (chilli oil) (optional)

Tan tan nabe, a Chinese-inspired miso-sesame hotpot with minced (ground) meat, is one of the most popular dishes from my first cookbook, *DONABE*. This version, made with soya milk, has a very different flavour profile and method. It's just as satisfying, with the extra richness of a creamy soya milk broth. Minced pork is seasoned with tobanjan (Chinese chilli bean paste) and aromatics, then layered with mushrooms, tofu, bean sprouts and pak choi (bok choi). The soya milk-miso broth is gently spicy, deeply flavourful and surprisingly light. It's quick to prepare and perfect for weeknights or casual gatherings at the table. Tan tan nabe

Pork is thought to replenish energy and supports skin health. Soya milk is believed to help cool internal heat and maintains moisture balance. This combination may support recovery from fatigue while promoting healthy skin and hydration from within.

EQUIPMENT: Classic-style donabe (or heavy duty pot) (1.8 litre/60 fl oz)

METHOD: To make the seasoned pork, heat the sesame oil in a small sauté pan over a medium heat. Add the garlic and ginger, and sauté until aromatic. Add the pork mince and cook until nearly done. Push the pork to one side of the pan and add the tobanjan to the empty space. Stir until fragrant, then mix with the pork. Add the sake and oyster sauce, and simmer for 1–2 minutes until the liquid is mostly reduced. Season with black pepper and remove from the heat.

To make the broth, whisk together the miso, sesame paste, dashi and soya milk in a bowl until smooth. Adjust the seasoning with salt, if needed.

Layer the shimeji mushrooms, tofu, enoki mushrooms, half of the seasoned meat and half of the bean sprouts in the donabe. Pour in the broth, cover and set over a medium-high heat. Bring to a simmer, about 10 minutes.

Add the remaining bean sprouts, pak choi and remaining seasoned meat. Bring it back to a simmer and cook for 1–2 more minutes, or until everything is tender.

Serve in individual bowls, garnished with the sesame seeds and spring onion, with la-yu, if desired.

FLAVOUR VARIATION: Instead of pork, chicken mince can also work well.

Marudori Nabe

SIMMERED WHOLE CHICKEN AND SOUP

丸鶏鍋

Serves 4–6

For the ginger lemon sauce

- ½ tbsp finely grated fresh root ginger
- ½ tbsp Shio-Koji (page 238)
- 2-3 tbsp lemon juice
- 1 spring onion (scallion), white part only, minced
- 1 tbsp extra virgin olive oil
- 1 tsp sliced dried chilli

For the spring onion shoyu sauce

- 3 tbsp shoyu (or tamari for gluten free)
- 1 tbsp raw brown sugar
- 1 tbsp kurozu (Japanese black vinegar)
- 1 tbsp toasted sesame oil
- 1 garlic clove, minced
- ½ tbsp minced fresh root ginger
- 2 spring onions (scallions), white parts only, minced
- la-yu (chilli oil), to taste
- 1 tbsp toasted white sesame seeds

For the donabe

- 4 dried shiitake mushrooms, quickly rinsed
- 1.5-1.8 kg (3 lb 5 oz-4 lb) whole chicken, cleaned
- 3 spring onions (scallions), green parts only
- 1 tbsp thinly sliced fresh root ginger
- 3-4 garlic cloves, peeled
- two 5 x 10 cm (2 x 4 in) pieces kombu
- 250 ml (8 fl oz/1 cup) sake
- water, as needed
- 200 g (7 oz) enoki mushrooms, trimmed
- 300 g (10½ oz) daikon (mooli), cut into 4 mm (¼ in) rounds, quartered or halved
- sea salt and freshly ground black pepper, to taste

This slow-cooked donabe dish is perfect for a cosy Sunday supper, especially to share with friends. A whole chicken simmers gently until meltingly tender and the broth becomes rich, deeply flavoured and full of natural nourishment from the bones and skin. I like serving it with two kinds of dipping sauces for different flavour variations throughout the meal – and the leftover soup makes a perfect shime (finishing course) with ramen, so make sure to save enough of it.

This soup is a classic for when you need a warm, healing boost. It is thougt that whole chicken helps build strength and stamina, while ginger, garlic and spring onion (scallion) warm the body and support your natural defences. It's the kind of dish that helps you stay well – or bounce back faster when you're feeling run down.

EQUIPMENT: Classic-style donabe (or heavy duty pot) (2.5 litre/85 fl oz)

METHOD: Prepare the sauces. Whisk together the ingredients for each sauce in two separate bowls.

Soak the dried shiitake in about 250 ml (8 fl oz/1 cup) water for about 2 hours, or until fully rehydrated and aromatic (if you are in a rush, use hot water and soak for about 30 minutes). Trim the stems and cut each mushroom in half if large. Reserve the soaking water.

To prepare the soup, place the whole chicken in a donabe. Add the shiitake, spring onion tops, ginger, garlic and kombu. Pour in the sake, reserved mushroom soaking water, plus enough water to cover the chicken. Cover and set over a medium-high heat and bring to the boil. Skim off any impurities or fat that rise to the surface, as needed. Reduce the heat to a gentle simmer and place a drop lid or baking parchment cartouche directly over the surface of the ingredients to help the broth circulate evenly. Simmer for about 45 minutes.

Add the enoki mushrooms and daikon, and continue to simmer for another 15–20 minutes, or until everything is cooked through and tender. Season the soup with salt and pepper.

Remove from the heat and let rest for 15–20 minutes before serving.

You can transfer the whole chicken to a serving platter or divide it directly in the donabe with a knife or kitchen scissors at the table. Enjoy with the dipping sauces and small cups of hot soup on the side.

Tamago Niku Dofu

QUICK SIMMERED AND EGG-COVERED BEEF AND TOFU

玉子肉豆腐

Serves 4

- 1 tbsp extra virgin olive oil
- 1 tbsp sesame oil
- 1 onion, thinly sliced
- 2 garlic cloves, thinly sliced
- 400 g (14 oz) thinly sliced beef
- 150 g (5½ oz) king oyster mushrooms, trimmed and cut into bite-size slices
- 30 ml (2 fl oz/¼ cup) sake
- 30 ml (2 fl oz/¼ cup) shoyu (or tamari for gluten free)
- 2 tbsp mirin
- 120 ml (4 fl oz/½ cup) Awase Dashi (page 233) or your choice of stock
- 300 g (10½ oz) medium-firm tofu, cubed
- 3 large eggs, beaten

To serve

- 1 spring onion (scallion), thinly sliced at an angle
- sliced dried chilli
- ground sansho (Japanese mountain pepper)

This comforting one-pot dish features thinly sliced beef and tofu gently simmered with onion, mushrooms and a shoyu-based broth, then finished with a soft layer of egg. I make it often in a tagine-style donabe – the shallow, wide base allows the ingredients to cook evenly over steady, focused heat. A regular frying pan (skillet) works well, too. The savoury-sweet flavours soak into the tofu and beef, and the silky egg brings it all together. It's a deeply satisfying dish, especially when served over warm rice to make a simple donburi.

Beef, tofu and egg are believed to work together to support stamina, nourish blood, and promote skin and muscle health. This gently warming dish may help restore balance when you're feeling drained – both physically and emotionally.

EQUIPMENT: Tagine-style donabe (or frying pan/skillet with a lid)

METHOD: Combine the olive oil, sesame oil, onion and garlic in a donabe and set over a medium heat. Sauté for about 5 minutes, or until the onion is soft and translucent.

Add the beef to the donabe and continue to sauté until the meat is mostly cooked through.

Add the mushrooms, sake, shoyu, mirin and dashi. Cover with the lid, increase the heat to medium-high and bring to a high simmer. Add the tofu and bring back to a high simmer.

Gradually pour the beaten eggs over the top in a circular motion. Cover, turn off the heat, and let rest for a couple of minutes, or until the egg is softly set to your liking.

Serve with the spring onion, sliced dried chilli and a sprinkle of sansho.

NOTE: You can substitute thinly sliced pork, chicken or even minced (ground) meat in place of the beef. Just be sure to adjust the cooking time slightly, depending on the cut and thickness.

Gyu-Maki Shabu Shabu

THINLY SLICED BEEF-WRAPPED WATERCRESS HOTPOT

クレソンの牛肉巻き
しゃぶしゃぶ

Serves 3–4

GF

For the hot goma dare (spicy sesame sauce)

2 tbsp white sesame paste (tahini can work too)
2 tbsp rice vinegar
90 ml (3 fl oz/⅓ cup) Kaeshi (page 239)
2 tsp la-yu (chilli oil), or more to taste

For the beef and watercress rolls

450 g (1 lb) beef shabu shabu slices (12–15 slices)
400 g (14 oz) watercress, cut into 10 cm (4 in) lengths

For the donabe

800 ml (27 fl oz/scant 3½ cups) Awase Dashi (page 233) or your choice of stock
90 ml (3 fl oz/⅓ cup) sake
1 tsp sea salt
4–5 cabbage leaves, cut into thin strips
2–3 garlic cloves, thinly sliced
1 small knob fresh root ginger, very finely julienned
150 g (5½ oz) oyster mushrooms, trimmed and cut into thin slices

My sister is a true champion of *omotenashi* – the Japanese spirit of welcoming others with warmth and care. Even while working full time and raising her son, she always made time to plan thoughtful menus and prepare beautiful meals that felt effortless and heartfelt. This dish is inspired by one of the many donabe dinners she made for me when I returned to Japan, where she wrapped watercress or enoki mushrooms in thinly sliced beef, steamed them simply and served with ponzu. My version is a quick simmered take, layered over cabbage and aromatics and enjoyed with hot goma dare (spicy sesame sauce) instead of ponzu.

EQUIPMENT: Classic-style donabe (or heavy duty pot) (2.5 litre/85 fl oz)

METHOD: To make the hot goma dare, whisk together the sesame paste and vinegar in a bowl, gradually adding the vinegar to prevent clumping. Whisk in the kaeshi and la-yu, to taste.

To make the beef rolls, lay out each slice of beef and place a small bundle of watercress near one end. Roll up the beef around the watercress, slightly overlapping as you go to secure it.

Set the donabe on a table-top stove. Combine the dashi, sake and salt in the donabe and bring to a high simmer over a medium-high heat. Add the cabbage, garlic, ginger and mushrooms, and bring back to a simmer.

Arrange the beef rolls on top of the vegetables in a circular pattern. Bring back to a simmer and cook for 2–3 minutes, or until the beef is just cooked through.

Cut each roll with kitchen scissors into 2–3 pieces, for easier bites when serving, if preferred. Enjoy the rolls and other cooked ingredients with the hot goma dare as a dipping sauce, or drizzle it over.

FLAVOUR VARIATION: You can wrap other ingredients in beef in place of watercress. I like using cut nagaimo (mountain yam), garlic chives or pea shoots – each bring a different texture and taste.

Adjust the amount of la-yu in the sauce according to your heat tolerance, or omit it completely, if you prefer.

→ Hotpot Gathering: Gyu-maki Watercress Shabu Shabu (page 142), Mushi-Zakana no Goma Abura Sauce (page 102), Satoimo no Tomo-Ae (page 53), Daikon Salad Shio-Koji Dressing-Ae (page 51), Ninjin Wakame Gohan (page 193)

Hana Shumai

STEAMED PORK AND LOTUS 'FLOWER' DUMPLINGS

花焼売

Serves 3–4

For the filling

400 g (14 oz) minced (ground) pork
½ tbsp finely grated fresh root ginger
¼ tsp raw brown sugar
¼ tsp sea salt
¼ tsp freshly ground black pepper
1 tbsp katakuriko (potato starch)
1 tsp shoyu (or tamari for gluten free)
1 tbsp sake
1½–2 tbsp beaten egg
1 tsp sesame oil
2 tbsp minced spring onions (scallions)
100 g (3½ oz) lotus root, coarsely minced

For steaming

1 package (20–24 pieces) shumai skins (thinner type preferred)
18–20 goji berries
napa cabbage leaves

To serve

shoyu (or tamari for gluten free)
kurozu (Japanese black vinegar) or rice vinegar
karashi (Japanese hot mustard)

Hana shumai, or flower dumplings, are a fun twist on the classic steamed pork dumpling. Shumai is a popular dish in Japan, originally adapted from Chinese shao mai. Instead of wrapping the filling in a square skin, the wrappers are finely shredded and tossed with the meat filling, giving each piece the look of a white chrysanthemum flower when steamed. A single goji berry on top adds a beautiful accent, like the centre of a blossom. Chopped lotus root mixed into the pork creates a crisp texture and makes each bite extra juicy. They're fun to eat and extra special when shared right out of the donabe at the table, so I recommend making an extra batch if you have hungry guests.

EQUIPMENT: Donabe steamer (or pot with a steam basket)

METHOD: To prepare the filling, combine all the ingredients, except for the spring onion and lotus root, in a bowl and knead until smooth but not sticky. Add the spring onion and lotus root and mix again until well combined. Cover the surface tightly with cling film (plastic wrap) and refrigerate for 30 minutes.

Cut the shumai skins into thin strips and gently fluff them in a shallow bowl.

To shape the shumai, take about 1½ tablespoons of the filling and roll into a ball in your hands. Repeat with the rest of the filling. You will have 18–20 balls. Toss each ball in the shredded shumai skins so the strips coat the surface. Top each with a goji berry and press gently so it stays in place.

Set up the donabe steamer and bring the water to the boil. Spread cabbage leaves on the steam grate, cover and steam for about 2 minutes until wilted. Dab any excess moisture from the surface, then arrange the shumai in a single layer on top. Cover and steam for 7–9 minutes over a medium-high heat, or until the shumai are cooked through. Cook in batches, depending on the size of your donabe steamer.

Each person can make their own dipping sauce by combining shoyu and kurozu to taste (I usually like a 1:1 ratio), and a dab of karashi on the side. Serve the hot shumai straight from the steamer and enjoy dipping each bite.

FLAVOUR VARIATION: For a gluten-free option, you can substitute the shredded shumai skins with finely shredded cabbage. The texture and look will be slightly different, but it's still delicious.

Spare Rib Oden

SIMMERED PORK SPARE RIB BROTH

スペアリブおでん

Serves 4

For the goma dare (sesame sauce)

60 ml (2 fl oz/¼ cup) mirin, boiled once
60 ml (2 fl oz/¼ cup) white sesame paste
2 tbsp shoyu (or tamari for gluten free)

For the donabe

750 g (1 lb 10 oz) pork ribs, separated
500 g (1 lb 2 oz) daikon (mooli), peeled thickly and cut into 3 cm (1 in) thick rounds
1 x 200 g (7 oz) block konnyaku (yam cake)
20–30 g (¾–1 oz) hayani-kombu (see Notes)
250 g (9 oz) boiled octopus legs
4 large eggs, soft-boiled and peeled

For the oden broth

1.5 litres (50 fl oz/6¼ cups) Awase Dashi (page 233)
75 ml (2½ fl oz/5 tbsp) sake
75 ml (2½ fl oz/5 tbsp) mirin
3 tbsp shoyu (or tamari for gluten free)
½ tsp sea salt, or more to taste

To serve

karashi (Japanese hot mustard paste)
yuzu-kosho (yuzu and green chilli pepper paste)
tororo kombu (vinegar-seasoned fluffy kombu)
thinly sliced spring onion (scallion)

This hearty oden brings together tender pork spare ribs and assorted ingredients, slowly simmered in a seasoned dashi broth. Spare ribs are not a traditional oden addition (fish cakes are more common), but I love how they become incredibly succulent and enrich the broth with deep flavour. There are no rules, so I encourage you to switch up the ingredients to cook in the broth to your style. Oden is a beloved dish in Japan, enjoyed at home, in restaurants and at street stalls, especially in winter. It's also a staple at *konbini* (convenience stores), where the warm, savoury aroma often greets you as soon as you walk in during the cold season. I like serving it with plain rice, and I always make extra – because leftover oden tastes even better the next day.

EQUIPMENT: Classic-style donabe (or heavy duty pot) (2.5 litre/85 fl oz)

METHOD: To make the goma dare, gradually whisk the once-boiled mirin into the sesame paste, then add the shoyu and mix until smooth.

Blanch the pork ribs in boiling water for 2 minutes. Drain, rinse briefly under running water, then drain again to remove impurities released from the pork.

Bevel the edges of the daikon slices, if desired. Simmer in water or steam for about 10 minutes, until par-cooked.

Score both sides of the konnyaku in a crosshatch pattern, cut into quarters, then slice each into triangles. Blanch for 2–3 minutes, then drain.

Soak the hayani-kombu until pliable, then cut into 15 cm (6 in) lengths and tie into knots.

Combine the ingredients for the oden broth in a donabe. Add the pork ribs, daikon and konnyaku, and bring to a high simmer over a medium-high heat. Reduce to a gentle simmer and place a drop lid or baking parchment cartouche directly on the surface of the ingredients to help the broth circulate evenly. Cook for about 45 minutes. (Optional: turn off the heat and let rest for 1 hour to deepen the flavour and tenderise the meat.)

Add the octopus (skewer or cut into bite-sized pieces), kombu knots and eggs. Simmer for a further 15–20 minutes, or until everything is tender and flavourful. Adjust the seasoning with more salt, if needed.

Serve directly from the donabe at the table. Each person can pick their favourite ingredients and enjoy with karashi, yuzu-kosho, tororo kombu (especially good on daikon) or spring onion, as toppings. Pour a little goma dare over the pork and other ingredients, if desired.

NOTES: I like using the leftover broth to cook flavoured rice the next day.

Hayani-kombu is quick-cooking kombu. If it is unavailable, you can substitute with wakame (rehydrated if using dried). Add it in the last 1–2 minutes of cooking, just before serving.

Niku Yasai Jeongol

KOREAN-INSPIRED SIZZLING BEEF AND COLOURFUL VEGETABLES

肉野菜ジョンゴル

Serves 4

GF

For the beef

- 1 tbsp gochujang, plus extra to serve (optional)
- ½ tbsp finely grated fresh root ginger
- 50 ml (1¾ fl oz/3½ tbsp) Kaeshi (page 239)
- 300 g (10½ oz) beef (flap meat/sirloin bavette or skirt steak), cut into thin strips

For the donabe

- 1 tbsp sesame oil
- 100 g (3½ oz) bean sprouts
- 100 g (3½ oz) garlic chives, cut into 7 cm (3 in) lengths
- 100 g (3½ oz) enoki mushrooms, trimmed
- 100 g (3½ oz) carrot, julienned into 7 cm (3 in) lengths
- 100 g (3½ oz) daikon (mooli), cut into 3 mm (⅛ in) rounds, then halved if needed
- 100 g (3½ oz) watercress, cut into 7 cm (3 in) lengths
- 3 large eggs
- 100 ml (3½ fl oz/scant ½ cup) Kaeshi (page 239), or to taste
- sliced dried chilli, to garnish

This dish is inspired by jeongol, a Korean hotpot where meat, vegetables and other ingredients are beautifully arranged in a shallow pot and simmered at the table in a lightly seasoned broth. My version is like a quick sukiyaki, with marinated beef and colourful vegetables sizzling in a wide tagine-style donabe. This is a very flexible recipe, as I often change it depending on the vegetables I have on hand. At the table, once everything is sizzling and the eggs are lightly set, I stir it all together quickly. It's a little spicy and deeply savoury from the kaeshi sauce, and perfect with freshly cooked plain rice.

EQUIPMENT: Tagine-style donabe (or frying pan/skillet with a lid)

METHOD: For the beef marinade, whisk together the gochujang, ginger and kaeshi in a bowl. Add the beef and mix well. Let marinate in the refrigerator for at least 30 minutes.

Spread the sesame oil across the bottom of a donabe. Arrange the bean sprouts evenly over the base, then neatly arrange the marinated beef, garlic chives, mushrooms, carrot, daikon and watercress in a radial pattern, like the spokes of a wheel, alternating the ingredients around the centre. Cover with the lid and set over a medium heat. When it begins to sizzle, about 2–3 minutes, continue cooking for another 5 minutes.

Make a small well in the centre. Crack the eggs into a cup, then gently pour them into the space, one at a time. Pour in about two-thirds of the kaeshi along the sides of the donabe. Cover again and cook for another 5 minutes, or until the beef and vegetables are cooked through and the eggs are set to your liking.

Remove from heat and bring to the table. Mix everything together with a large spoon. Add more kaeshi, if needed. Garnish with sliced dried chilli and serve in individual bowls. Add more gochujang, if desired.

NOTE: For a milder version, omit the gochujang and sliced dried chilli, and replace the gochujang with a small amount of miso – this keeps the depth and umami without the heat.

Goma Nabe

SESAME HOTPOT

胡麻鍋

Serves 4

For the sesame broth base

60 ml (2 fl oz/¼ cup) white sesame paste
2 tbsp miso
2 tbsp shoyu (or tamari for gluten free)
½ tsp sea salt
60 ml (2 fl oz/¼ cup) sake

For the pork meatballs

450 g (1 lb) minced (ground) pork
1 large egg
1 tbsp katakuriko (potato starch)
1 tbsp finely grated fresh root ginger
1 tsp shoyu (or tamari for gluten free)
½ tsp sea salt
¼ tsp freshly ground black pepper
½ tsp sesame oil
1 tbsp extra virgin olive oil

For the donabe

150 g (5½ oz) soybean sprouts
300 g (10½ oz) daikon (mooli), cut into 5 mm (¼ in) rounds, then quartered or halved
6 medium napa cabbage leaves, cut into bite-size pieces
1 tbsp very finely julienned fresh root ginger
800 ml (27 fl oz/scant 3½ cups) Awase Dashi (page 233)
100 g (3 ½ oz) shimeji mushrooms, trimmed
1 small carrot, julienned
100 g (3½ oz) watercress
4 tbsp ground white sesame seeds
1 tsp Sichuan peppercorns, coarsely ground (optional)
½ tsp sliced dried chilli
la-yu (chilli oil), to serve

A nutty sesame broth forms the base of this hotpot, where tender meatballs and vegetables soak up layers of flavour. Browning the meatballs before adding them to the broth brings extra depth and richness, and it's well worth the extra step, although it's not necessary. For a fragrant finish, use freshly toasted and ground sesame seeds just before serving. I love finishing this dish with ramen noodles for the shime (finishing course) – topped with a generous amount of thinly sliced spring onions (scallions) for a simple, satisfying end.

Pork is believed to help replenish energy and build strength. It is said sesame supports blood and circulation, while ginger warms and aids digestion. Together, they gently restore the body and boost stamina – perfect for chilly days.

EQUIPMENT: Classic-style donabe (or heavy duty pot) (2.5 litre/85 fl oz)

METHOD: Whisk together the ingredients for the sesame broth base in a bowl.

Combine all the ingredients for the meatballs, except for the olive oil, in a bowl. Knead until smooth. Cover the surface tightly with cling film (plastic wrap) and let rest in the refrigerator for 30 minutes.

Form the meat into about 12 balls by hand. Heat the olive oil in a sauté pan over a medium-high heat and add the meatballs. Cook until lightly golden, 2–3 minutes per side. They don't need to be cooked through.

Spread the soybean sprouts in a donabe, followed by the daikon, cabbage and ginger. Pour in the dashi, cover and bring to a high simmer over a medium-high heat. Reduce the heat to a simmer, and cook for 2–3 minutes.

Add the shimeji mushrooms and browned meatballs to the donabe, then pour in the sesame broth base. Add the carrot, then cover again. Cook for 3–5 minutes, or until the meatballs are cooked through.

Add the watercress and let it wilt, then sprinkle in the sesame seeds, Sichuan peppercorns (if using) and sliced dried chilli. Drizzle with la-yu and serve immediately.

FLAVOUR VARIATIONS: Switch to your choice of minced (ground) meat (beef, chicken or lamb) for a change. You can also enjoy this broth with seafood or keep it vegan with plant-based ingredients.

Kurozu Sanratan Nabe

SWEET AND SOUR MINCED PORK HOTPOT

黒酢酸辣湯鍋

Serves 2

GF
OP

1 tbsp sesame oil
1 garlic clove, minced
½ tbsp finely julienned fresh root ginger
220 g (8 oz) minced (ground) pork
1 tsp tobanjan (Chinese chilli bean paste)
5 g (⅛ oz) dried wood ear mushrooms, rehydrated and cut into bite-size pieces
600 ml (20 fl oz/2½ cups) Tori Dashi (page 236) or your choice of stock
2 tbsp sake
1½ tbsp usukuchi shoyu
1 tbsp oyster sauce
200 g (7 oz) soft tofu, cut into small cubes
1 tbsp katakuriko (potato starch), dissolved in 2 tbsp water
100 g (3½ oz) bean sprouts
100 g (3½ oz) garlic chives, cut into 5 cm (2 in) lengths
2 large eggs, beaten
1–2 tbsp kurozu (Japanese black vinegar) or rice vinegar
sea salt and freshly ground black pepper, to taste

To serve

minced spring onion (scallion)
la-yu (chilli oil) (optional)

Sanrantan is a popular hot and sour soup in Japan, originally adapted from the classic Chinese soup suan la tang. I love turning it into a cosy donabe hotpot, with ground pork, tofu and vegetables simmered in a tangy, spicy broth. Kurozu (Japanese black vinegar) adds mellow acidity and depth, while tobanjan (Chinese chilli bean paste) brings gentle heat. Even with a small donabe, I still like to enjoy a shime (finishing course) with the remaining broth with some extra added. Glass noodles are my favourite shime for this dish. This hotpot may help support the body's natural immune defences and rebuild energy to protect against colds and seasonal fatigue.

EQUIPMENT: Classic-style donabe (or heavy duty pot) (1.8 litre/60 fl oz)

METHOD: Heat the sesame oil in a donabe over a medium heat. Add the garlic and ginger, and sauté until aromatic, then add the pork and cook until nearly done. Push the pork to one side of the donabe and add the tobanjan to the empty space. Stir until fragrant, then mix with the pork. Add the mushrooms and stir.

Pour in the dashi, sake, usukuchi shoyu and oyster sauce, then add the tofu. Bring to a high simmer over a medium-high heat. Adjust the seasoning with salt, if needed.

Stir the katakuriko slurry together and gradually add it to the broth while stirring. Stir gently until the broth is slightly thickened. Add the bean sprouts and garlic chives, and bring back to a high simmer.

Gradually pour in the beaten eggs in a circular motion. Wait about 30 seconds, then gently stir. Season with black pepper and drizzle in the kurozu to finish.

Serve hot, garnished with spring onion and a drizzle of la-yu, if desired.

NOTE: For a gluten-free version, replace the usukuchi shoyu with ½ tablespoon of tamari and ⅓ teaspoon or more of sea salt.

FLAVOUR VARIATION: Instead of pork, chicken mince can also work well.

Gyu Touchi-Mushi

STEAMED FERMENTED BLACK BEAN BEEF WITH SWEET RICE AND KABOCHA

牛肉の豆豉蒸し

Serves 3–4

GF

For the touchi sauce

- 1½ tbsp touchi (fermented Chinese black beans), coarsely minced
- 2 tbsp shoyu (or tamari for gluten free)
- ½ tbsp Okinawa black sugar (can substitute raw brown sugar)
- 1 tbsp Shaoxing rice wine or sake
- 1 garlic clove, finely grated
- ½ tbsp finely grated fresh root ginger
- 1 tsp sliced dried chilli

For steaming

- 350 g (12 oz) beef, cut across the grain into bite-size strips (flap meat/sirloin bavette or skirt steak preferred)
- 3 tbsp glutinous (sweet) rice
- ½ tsp ground sansho (Japanese mountain pepper)
- 450 g (1 lb) kabocha squash, peeled and cut into 2 cm (¾ in) thick wedges

To serve

- minced chives

This dish is inspired by Chinese steamed meat dishes, which often feature marinated meat and touchi (fermented Chinese black bean) flavours. It's so easy to make in a donabe, and the flavour combination is incredibly satisfying. Thinly sliced beef is marinated in a rich touchi sauce, then mixed with sansho-spiced sweet rice and steamed over a bed of tender kabocha squash. The beef turns juicy and full of umami, while the sticky rice absorbs all the rich, aromatic flavours. Sweet kabocha balances everything with its natural tenderness. I usually use flap meat (sirloin bavette) or skirt steak, but other cuts like boneless short rib or ribeye can work well too. I like to serve this dish with a light green salad to make it a comforting and complete meal.

EQUIPMENT: Donabe steamer (or pot with a steam basket), heatproof shallow bowl (about 20 cm/8 in in diameter)

METHOD: Whisk together the ingredients for the sauce in a bowl. Add the beef and let marinate for at least 30 minutes, or preferably 2–3 hours, in the refrigerator.

Soak the sweet rice in water for 30 minutes, then drain.

Set up the donabe steamer and bring the water to the boil.

Combine the marinated beef, rice and ground sansho in a bowl and mix well.

Line the bottom of a heatproof shallow bowl with the kabocha, then spread the beef and rice mixture evenly over the top.

Place the bowl on the steam grate of the donabe, cover and steam over a medium heat for about 30 minutes, or until the beef and rice are fully cooked and the kabocha is tender.

Sprinkle with minced chives and serve.

FLAVOUR VARIATION: Instead of beef, I also like pork shoulder/butt or chicken thigh (cut into bite-size pieces). They come out juicy and flavourful, too.

Tori Amazake Nabe

CHICKEN AMAZAKE HOTPOT

鶏の甘酒鍋

Serves 3–4

This protein-rich hotpot features a gently savoury miso broth enriched with fresh ginger and amazake (sweet fermented rice drink). It is thought to help with rebalancing and glow, especially in colder seasons or when feeling run down. The chicken is prepared in two ways – thigh meat is cubed and minced (ground) chicken is made into meatballs with aromatic chopped shiso, making the dish extra tasty. Amazake is added at the end, so it brings a fresh and subtle roundness and depth (and it's rich in natural probiotics). It's a versatile recipe – you can substitute the chicken with more vegetables or even seafood to make it your own. For the shime (finishing course), I like to add kishimen (flat udon) into the remaining broth and topped with shredded nori, but other noodles or rice are also good.

For the chicken

- 300 g (10½ oz) skinless, boneless chicken thighs, cut into bite-size pieces
- ½ tsp sea salt, divided
- 300 g (10½ oz) minced (ground) chicken
- tbsp katakuriko (potato starch)
- tsp finely grated fresh root ginger
- tbsp sake
- tbsp beaten egg
- tsp freshly ground black pepper
- 0-15 shiso leaves, chopped

For the donabe

- 00 ml (20 fl oz/2½ cups) Awase Dashi (page 233)
- tbsp sake
- tsp sea salt
- -5 napa cabbage leaves, cut into bite-size pieces
- 00 g (7 oz) satsumaimo (Japanese sweet potato), peeled and diced
- tbsp miso
- tbsp very finely julienned fresh root ginger
- 00 g (7 oz) medium-firm tofu, cut into 6-8 pieces
- 00 g (3½ oz) shimeji mushrooms, trimmed
- 00 g (3½ oz) enoki mushrooms, trimmed
- tbsp Amazake (page 240)
- 0 g (2 oz) mizuna (mustard greens), chopped

To serve

- uzu zest
- hichimi togarashi (Japanese seven spice powder) (optional)

EQUIPMENT: Classic-style donabe (or heavy duty pot) (2.5 litre/85 fl oz)

METHOD: Season both sides of the chicken thighs with 1 teaspoon salt and let rest in the refrigerator for at least 30 minutes, or 2–3 hours, if possible.

Combine the chicken mince, ½ teaspoon salt, katakuriko, ginger, sake, egg and black pepper in a bowl. Knead well. Add the chopped shiso and knead again until thoroughly mixed. Form into 8–10 balls.

Set the donabe on a table-top stove. Add the dashi and heat over a medium-high heat. Add the sake and salt, then add the napa cabbage and satsumaimo. Cover and bring to a high simmer. Add both kinds of chicken, bring back to a high simmer, then reduce the heat to a simmer. Cook for 2–3 minutes.

Add the miso and ginger and stir to dissolve, then add the tofu and both kinds of mushrooms. Cover again and bring back to a simmer, cook for a 2–3 minutes, or until everything is cooked through.

To finish, stir in the amazake and adjust the seasoning with more salt, if needed. Add the mizuna and let it wilt. Sprinkle with some yuzu zest.

Serve in individual bowls, and enjoy with some shichimi togarashi on the side, if desired.

FLAVOUR VARIATION: To make this vegan, simply omit the chicken and use a plant-based dashi. Hearty vegetables like kabocha squash, daikon (mooli) or carrots work beautifully in its place.

Tori Lemon Joya Nabe

CHICKEN FILLETS, SPINACH AND LEMON HOTPOT

鶏肉とレモンの常夜鍋

Serves 2–3

For the tamari-lemon dipping sauce

2 tbsp grain mustard
2 tbsp lemon juice
60 ml (2 fl oz/¼ cup) tamari
2 tbsp extra virgin olive oil
1 spring onion (scallion), thinly sliced

For the broth

4 tbsp Saikyo miso or other sweet white miso
120 ml (4 fl oz/½ cup) sake
500 ml (17 fl oz/generous 2 cups) Awase Dashi (page 233) or your choice of stock

For the donabe

300 g (10½ oz) mini chicken fillets (tenders), thinly sliced at an angle
1 tsp sea salt
1 tbsp katakuriko (potato starch)
150 g (5½ oz) kabocha squash, peeled and cut into bite-size pieces
2 garlic cloves, thinly sliced
200 g (7 oz) enoki mushrooms, trimmed
200 g (7 oz) spinach, cut into 5 cm (2 in) lengths
a few thin lemon slices
1 tbsp toasted white sesame seeds

Joya nabe is a popular hotpot dish in Japan, typically made with thinly sliced pork and spinach simmered in dashi and enjoyed with ponzu. The name *joya* (常夜) comes from the idea that it's so simple and good, you could enjoy it every night without getting tired of it. Instead of pork, I like to use chicken fillets (tenders) for their lightness and clean flavour, which goes well with a hint of lemon. The broth is lightly seasoned with Saikyo miso and sake for a soft aromatic depth, with thinly sliced garlic for extra warmth. I like to serve it also with a tangy tamari-lemon dipping sauce for a refreshing touch. For shime (finishing course), I often enjoy a quick ojiya (rice soup) or toss in some rice noodles to end the meal.

It is said that chicken supports stamina and gentle recovery, garlic warms and refreshes the body, while spinach nourishes the blood and promotes healthy skin. Lemon adds a bright, cleansing effect and is believed to help support natural collagen production. This clean, soothing hotpot may help keep the body energised and the skin vibrant from the inside out.

EQUIPMENT: Classic-style donabe (or heavy duty pot) (1.8 litre/60 fl oz)

METHOD: Whisk together the ingredients for the dipping sauce in a small bowl.

Whisk together the ingredients for the broth in a separate bowl.

Dust the chicken slices evenly with sea salt and katakuriko.

Add the kabocha, garlic and mushrooms to a donabe. Pour in the broth, cover with the lid and bring to a high simmer over a medium-high heat. Reduce to a simmer and cook for 2–3 minutes, or until the kabocha is almost cooked through.

Add the chicken, spinach and lemon slices, and continue to cook until the chicken is cooked through. Sprinkle with the toasted sesame seeds.

Serve at the table. For the first round, each person can take a few cooked ingredients into their own bowl of dipping sauce, or drizzle the sauce over. For the second or later round, enjoy with the broth. This is not a firm rule, however!

FLAVOUR VARIATIONS: You can swap chicken fillets (tenders) for other cuts of meat, or tofu for a plant-based version. Sometimes I make it with Western vegetable stock or consommé instead of dashi, and it's also delicious.

You can also enjoy this dish with Kaeshi Ponzu (page 239).

VI

RICE & NOODLES

Rice is the foundation of Japanese cuisine, and for me, it's hard to imagine daily life without it. The purest way to enjoy rice is simply plain, with no seasonings or toppings, to savour its natural flavour. Even within short-grain rice, there's incredible variety depending on the grower, region and harvest year. Every autumn (fall), the first harvest is especially celebrated for its shiny, vibrant grains. Noodles are also deeply rooted in Japanese food culture, with soba, udon and ramen enjoyed across the country. While pasta and grains like quinoa aren't traditional, they have become familiar parts of everyday home cooking. In this chapter, I introduce donabe dishes that celebrate rice, noodles and other grains – including many easy one-pot meals that bring comfort and variety to the table.

Cooking Rice in Donabe

Rice cooked in a donabe is truly special. In recent years, more people in Japan have been rediscovering this traditional method, even moving away from modern electric rice cookers in favour of donabe. The gentle way a donabe builds heat and slowly steams after turning off the heat makes rice extra shiny, with perfect moisture and chewiness.

You can cook rice in any donabe with enough depth, but there are also donabe specifically designed for rice. The one I use is the original double-lid donabe rice cooker by Nagatani-en from Iga, Japan. Its thick, porous body and unique double-lid design create ideal heat circulation and let the donabe breathe as it cooks and rests. The result is fluffy rice with a naturally sweet aroma and flavour. This has been my daily ritual for many years and I still get excited every time I open the lid when the rice is ready.

Most of the rice recipes in this book are made with a double-lid donabe rice cooker (3 rice-cup size/1.5 litre/50 fl oz). But if you're using a classic-style donabe or even a regular pot (such as an enamelled cast-iron one), I've included simple adjustment notes, under Basic Rice Cooking Methods (pages 170–171), so you can still make delicious rice your way.

TYPES OF RICE

The most common rice used in Japanese cooking is short-grain rice, known for its shiny appearance, aroma and chewy texture. There are many varieties, but I typically use the Koshihikari variety, which is popular and easy to find where I live. In the UK and US, short-grain rice is often labelled 'sushi rice', although in Japanese, 'sushi rice' simply refers to rice seasoned with vinegar for sushi. If you're able to find the harvest year or milled/polished date on the package, choose the one closest to your purchase date for the freshest result.

WATER FOR COOKING RICE

Short-grain rice cooks best with soft, cold or cool water. Filtered water or soft mineral water is ideal for bringing out rice's natural sweetness and texture.

RICE MEASUREMENT

Rice has played such an important role in Japanese culture that we still use a traditional measurement dating back to the Edo period (1600s). At that time, rice was even used as a form of tax. The unit is called *go* (合). To this day, 1 go (or 1 rice cup) equals 180 ml (6 fl oz).

RICE AND WATER RATIO

For white rice, the standard ratio of rice to water is 9:10. For example, 1 rice cup (180 ml/6 fl oz) to 200 ml (7 fl oz) water. This can be adjusted depending on the variety, age of the rice, or your personal preference. Some people like firmer rice, while others prefer it more moist. Fresh crop rice usually contains more moisture, so in that case, the ratio can be closer to 1:1. For wholegrain brown rice, each rice cup (180 ml/6 fl oz) requires 250–300 ml (8–10 fl oz) water. There are also partially polished brown rice or other varieties, so I suggest referring to the package information.

ADDING OTHER GRAINS

When I cook white rice, whether plain or seasoned, I often like to add other grains. They bring extra layers of flavour, texture, colour and nutrients. I encourage you to play around and find combinations you enjoy. Some of my staples are mochi mugi (pearled barley), black rice (forbidden rice), quinoa and red rice. There are also convenient single-use multigrain rice mixes available at many markets. When adding grains, I typically add about 30–50 g (1–1¾ oz) to 2–3 rice cups of short-grain white rice, along with extra water. Check the package instructions for how much extra water is needed, as it can vary depending on the grain.

STORING RICE

For the best flavour, try to buy only the amount you can consume within a couple of months after opening (although up to several months is still fine). Once opened, store the rice to minimise oxidation. Keep it in an airtight container in the refrigerator (that's what I do), or in a cool, dry pantry away from sunlight and humidity.

BASIC RICE
COOKING METHODS

Shiro Gohan

Here is the basic white rice cooking method I use as a foundation.

EQUIPMENT: Double-lid donabe rice cooker (or heavy duty pot)

PLAIN WHITE RICE

白ごはん

Serves 5–6

3 Japanese rice cups (540 ml/18½ fl oz/2⅓ cups) short-grain white rice
600 ml (20 fl oz/2½ cups) water

IF USING A DOUBLE-LID DONABE RICE COOKER: Rinse the rice gently in a bowl with cold water by swirling it with your hand, then discard the water. Repeat a few times until the water becomes mostly clear. Drain completely.

Transfer the rice to the donabe and add the water. Let the rice soak for 20–30 minutes.

Cover with both lids and set over a medium-high heat. Once you see steady steam puffing from the top lid hole (usually after about 11–13 minutes), continue cooking for about 2 more minutes.

Turn off the heat and let it rest with both lids on for 20 minutes.

Uncover and gently fluff the rice with a rice paddle.

IF USING A CLASSIC-STYLE DONABE OR OTHER POT: After soaking the rice, cover with the lid and cook over a medium-high heat until it comes to the boil (this usually takes about 7–8 minutes). Once boiling, reduce the heat to low and continue cooking for 7–10 minutes, or until the water is mostly absorbed. You can briefly lift the lid to check. When the rice is ready to rest, you may hear a faint crackling sound. Turn off the heat and let it sit, covered, for 15–20 minutes. These timings are based on 3 rice cups of short-grain rice and may vary depending on your pot and the amount of rice.

NOTES: If you prefer a lightly crispy bottom to your rice (okoge), extend the cooking time by 1–2 minutes before turning off the heat.

If cooking with the double-lid donabe rice cooker, the inner lid has two holes and outer lid has one hole. Place the outer lid so that its hole positions perpendicular with the two holes of the inner lid below. This will create ideal pressure with the steam during cooking.

FLAVOUR VARIATION: To make Zakkoku Gohan (Plain White Rice with Multigrain Mix; pictured on page 167), add 2 tablespoons of multi-grain mix and 2–3 tablespoons of water to the measured rice and water, and cook as instructed above.

Genmai

PLAIN WHOLEGRAIN BROWN RICE

玄米ご飯

Serves 5–6

3 Japanese rice cups (540 ml/18½ fl oz/2⅓ cups) short wholegrain brown rice, rinsed and drained
750 ml (25 fl oz/3 cups) water, plus more for soaking
good pinch sea salt

Cooking wholegrain brown rice in a donabe takes time – both for soaking and cooking – but it's totally worth it. The result is tender and chewy without becoming mushy, with a subtle nutty aroma. I used to cook it in the soaking water, but I've found that replacing it with fresh water gives a more pristine flavour and helps remove any impurities released during soaking.

EQUIPMENT: Double-lid donabe rice cooker (or heavy duty pot)

IF USING A DOUBLE-LID DONABE RICE COOKER: Rinse the rice gently in a bowl with cold water by swirling it with your hand, then discard the water. Repeat a few times until the water becomes mostly clear. Drain completely.

In a bowl, combine the brown rice with about twice as much water. Soak in a cool place or in the refrigerator for 6–12 hours.

Drain and transfer the rice to the donabe. Add the measured water and the salt (adding the salt helps remove bitterness from the rice). Cover with both lids and set over a medium-high heat. Once you see steady steam puffing from the top lid hole (usually after about 15–18 minutes), continue cooking for another 15–18 minutes, or until the water is mostly absorbed. You can briefly lift the lids to check, if needed. You can also listen for a shift in sound – while the rice is cooking, it makes a bubbling sound, and as it nears readiness, the sound becomes softer and quieter.

Turn off the heat and let it rest for 30–40 minutes.

Uncover and gently fluff the rice with a rice paddle.

IF USING A CLASSIC-STYLE DONABE OR OTHER POT: After the ingredients are in the donabe, cover with the lid and cook over a medium heat until it comes to the boil (this may take 15–20 minutes). Once boiling, reduce the heat to low and continue cooking for about 25 minutes, or until the water is mostly absorbed. You can briefly lift the lid to check, if needed. When the rice is ready to rest, you may hear a faint crackling sound. Turn off the heat and let it sit, covered, for 15–20 minutes. These timings are based on 3 rice cups of short wholegrean brown rice and may vary depending on your pot and the amount of rice.

NOTE: Cooking time and rice/water ratio may vary, depending on the brand and amount of brown rice you cook, so you can try a few times to find the optimal way for you.

Lu Rou Fan

TAIWANESE-STYLE BRAISED PORK OVER RICE
魯肉飯

Serves 3–4

For the tamari-marinated eggs

- 2 tbsp sake, boiled once
- 2 tbsp tamari
- 2 tsp Okinawa black sugar or raw brown sugar
- 1 tsp kurozu (Japanese black vinegar)
- ¼ tsp Chinese five spice powder
- ½ star anise
- 4 large eggs (cold from the refrigerator), boiled for 7 minutes and peeled

For the donabe

- 2 dried shiitake mushrooms, quickly rinsed
- 200 ml (7 fl oz/scant 1 cup) water, or more as needed
- 450 g (1 lb) pork belly, in one piece
- 2 tbsp sesame oil
- 1 red onion, minced
- 2 garlic cloves, minced
- 1 tbsp minced fresh root ginger
- pinch of sea salt
- 2 tbsp Okinawa black sugar or raw brown sugar
- 120 ml (4 fl oz/½ cup) Shaoxing rice wine or sake
- 3 tbsp tamari
- 2 star anise
- ½ tsp Chinese five spice powder

To serve

- Plain White Rice (page 170), freshly cooked
- fresh coriander (cilantro) leaves
- pickled ginger shreds (from a jar)
- la-yu (chilli oil)

Lu rou fan, a beloved Taiwanese comfort food of braised pork over rice, has been a bit of an obsession for me – and something I always look forward to when I visit Taipei. This is my homage, made in a donabe, where pork belly becomes tender and deeply flavourful. I caramelise red onion slowly, add minced shiitake, and simmer it all with black sugar, tamari and sake for a hearty yet clean taste. The flavour becomes so deep that fried shallots, often added in the traditional version, aren't even necessary here. I like serving this dish with tamari-marinated eggs, pickled ginger, fresh herbs and a drizzle of la-yu (chilli oil) for a full, satisfying bowl. It's a great dish to make extra (I often double the recipe) and ahead for gatherings – the flavours only get better after resting.

EQUIPMENT: Classic-style donabe (or heavy duty pot) (1.2 litre/40 fl oz)

METHOD: To make the tamari-marinated eggs, combine all the ingredients, except the eggs, in a resealable plastic bag. Add the eggs and gently seal, removing as much air as possible. Marinate in the refrigerator for 6–24 hours.

Soak the dried shiitake in the water for about 2 hours, or until fully rehydrated and aromatic. Trim the stems and cut each shiitake into 3 mm (⅛ in) dice. Strain and reserve the soaking water.

Cut three-quarters of the pork into 1 cm (½ in) cubes and the rest into 3 mm (⅛ in) dice.

Heat the sesame oil in a donabe over a moderate heat. Add the onion, garlic, ginger and salt. Sauté until the onion is becoming caramelised and very soft, about 20–25 minutes. Add the mushrooms and cook for another 2 minutes. Stir occasionally to prevent burning.

Increase the heat to medium-high. Add the pork and sauté for a few minutes until lightly browned. Add the sugar and stir to coat for 1–2 minutes. Add the rice wine, tamari, reserved soaking water and star anise. Bring to the boil, then reduce to a low simmer. Skim off any foam or excess oil. Place a baking parchment cartouche directly over the surface of the liquid to help the broth circulate evenly and cover with the lid. Simmer for 45–60 minutes, or until the sauce is thicker and stew-like.

Add the Chinese five spice powder. Stir well and turn off the heat. Let rest for 15 minutes or longer before serving.

To serve, scoop some rice into bowls and spoon the stewed pork over the top. Top each with a tamari-marinated egg, some coriander leaves and pickled ginger. Drizzle with la-yu, to taste.

Ume Iwashi Takikomi Gohan

SARDINE AND PICKLED PLUM RICE

梅干しと鰯のオイル漬けの炊き込みご飯

Serves 4–5

- 2½ Japanese rice cups (450 ml/15 fl oz/scant 2 cups) short-grain white rice, rinsed
- 400 ml (14 fl oz/generous 1½ cups) Awase Dashi (page 233) or your choice of stock
- 2 tbsp sake
- ½ tbsp shoyu (or tamari for gluten free)
- 30 g (1 oz) fresh root ginger, finely julienned
- 200 g (7 oz) tinned sardines in oil (save 2 tbsp of the oil and drain the rest)
- 3 umeboshi (pickled plums), deseeded

To serve

- minced chives
- ground sansho (Japanese mountain pepper)

Tinned sardines in oil are great to keep in your pantry. They are ready to use and rich in umami and nutrients. I sometimes enjoy them straight from the can. This rice dish is incredibly easy to make: simply top the rice with sardines, umeboshi (pickled plums) and a few aromatics before cooking. Umeboshi bring balance with their salty umami and refreshing acidity, pairing perfectly with the richness of sardines. Be sure to include a little of the oil from the can, as it's packed with flavour. When serving, I highly recommend sprinkling ground sansho for a citrussy, numbing kick that complements the dish beautifully.

Sardines are traditionally believed to nourish the blood and support brain health, umeboshi aid digestion and detoxify, while ginger warms the body. This dish may help refresh energy and promote a clean, balanced feeling inside.

EQUIPMENT: Double-lid donabe rice cooker (or heavy duty pot)

METHOD: Combine the rice, dashi, sake and shoyu in a donabe. Let the rice soak for 20 minutes.

Spread the ginger evenly over the rice. Arrange the sardines neatly on top like a wheel, then add 2 tablespoons of the oil from the tins. Place the umeboshi on top. Cover the donabe with both lids and cook over a medium-high heat for 13–15 minutes, or until 2–3 minutes after the steam starts puffing out of the top lid. (If cooking with a classic-style donabe or other pot, see Basic Rice Cooking Methods on page 170.)

Turn off the heat and let it rest for 20 minutes.

Uncover and mix thoroughly. Garnish with chives and sprinkle with ground sansho before serving.

Corn Shio-Kombu Gohan

CORN AND SHIO-KOMBU RICE
とうもろこしと
塩昆布の炊き込みご飯

Serves 4–5

2 Japanese rice cups (360 ml/12 fl oz/1½ cups) short-grain white rice, rinsed
360 ml (12 fl oz/1½ cups) water or your choice of stock
15 g (½ oz) shio-kombu (seasoned shredded kelp)
kernels from 1–1½ corn-on-the-cobs
2 tbsp coconut butter (creamed whole coconut), softened

Corn rice is one of the donabe dishes I make most often in summer, and over the years, I've come up with many variations. With the umami-rich addition of shio-kombu (seasoned kelp), this version quickly became a favourite at home. Kombu is thought to gently cool and refresh, leaving the body light and balanced, especially on a warm day. I often love adding butter, but when I swapped it for coconut butter one night, it turned out amazing – the sweet corn and gentle coconut aroma work beautifully together. These ingredients bring so much flavour that I usually cook the rice with just water, but sometimes I use dashi or vegetable stock for a different flavour profile.

EQUIPMENT: Double-lid donabe rice cooker (or heavy duty pot)

METHOD: Combine the rice and water in a donabe. Let the rice soak for 20 minutes.

Spread the shio-kombu evenly over the rice, followed by the corn kernels. Cover the donabe with both lids and cook over a medium-high heat for 13–15 minutes, or until 2–3 minutes after the steam starts puffing out of the top lid. (If cooking with a classic-style donabe or other pot, see Basic Rice Cooking Methods on page 170.)

Turn off the heat and let it rest for 20 minutes.

Uncover and add the coconut butter, then fluff gently with a rice paddle, so it melts and mixes thoroughly with the rice.

NOTE: To soften the solid coconut butter, I usually put it in a small ceramic saucer and set on top of the donabe's lid when turning off the heat. During the resting time, it softens perfectly.

FLAVOUR VARIATION: Add about 60 g (2 oz/¼ cup) mochi mugi (pearled barley) and increase the water by about 120 ml (4 fl oz/½ cup) for extra texture and a nutty flavour. You can also use a vegetable dashi bag instead of plain water; tear it open and add about half of its contents to the water before cooking. It's an easy way to add more depth.

→ A Donburi Meal:
Soboro Oyako Don (page 191),
Hakusai Asa-Zuke (page 55),
Lentil Daikon Miso-Shiru
(page 90), Sayaingen Kurumi
Miso-Ae (page 41)

Niku Gohan

BEEF RICE
肉ご飯

Serves 4–5

For the beef marinade

- 250 g (9 oz) beef (hanger steak or your preferred cut), thinly cut into bite-size pieces
- 2 tbsp sake
- 2 tbsp shoyu (or tamari for gluten free)
- 1 tsp finely grated fresh root ginger
- 1 tbsp Okinawa black sugar or raw brown sugar

For the donabe

- 2 Japanese rice cups (360 ml/12 fl oz/1½ cups) short-grain rice, rinsed
- 300 ml (10 fl oz/1¼ cups) Awase Dashi (page 233) or water
- 1 tbsp shoyu (or tamari for gluten free)
- 60 g (2 oz) burdock root or parsnip, thinly shaved
- 1 medium carrot, julienned
- handful of basil leaves or your choice of herbs, to serve
- freshly ground black pepper, to taste

This beef rice is what I crave when I need stamina – it's hearty, satisfying and full of flavour. The rice soaks up all the richness from the beef and the donabe brings everything together beautifully. The hand-cut, briefly marinated beef becomes so tender after being cooked in a donabe. Sometimes I make it with just water instead of dashi, and it still tastes amazing. Basil adds a sweet, refreshing note that brightens the rich beef. Feel free to use your favourite herb to finish. A bowl of light soup and a fresh salad make it a complete and satisfying meal.

Beef is believed to nourish the blood and restores energy. It is thought that burdock promotes digestion, ginger boosts warmth, and basil refreshes the appetite and *qi* (vital energy). This dish may help build steady strength and keep digestion clear and balanced.

EQUIPMENT: Double-lid donabe rice cooker (or heavy duty pot)

METHOD: Combine the beef with the sake, shoyu, ginger and sugar in a bowl. Mix well and let it marinate for 15–30 minutes.

Combine the rice, dashi and shoyu in a donabe. Let the rice soak for 20 minutes.

Add the burdock root and spread evenly over the rice, followed by the carrot. Top with the marinated beef and any remaining marinade. Cover the donabe with both lids and cook over a medium-high heat for 13–15 minutes, or until 2–3 minutes after the steam starts puffing out of the top lid. (If cooking with a classic-style donabe or other pot, see Basic Rice Cooking Methods on page 170.)

Turn off the heat and let it rest for 20 minutes.

Uncover and add a good handful of basil and some black pepper. Fluff gently with a rice paddle.

FLAVOUR VARIATION: I sometimes swap regular shoyu with smoked shoyu for a nice smoky flavour. You can usually find smoked shoyu at speciality stores.

Takikomi Salmon Quinoa

FLUFFY QUINOA WITH SALMON, KALE AND MUSHROOMS

鮭とキヌアの炊き込み、
柚子胡椒風味

Serves 3–4

1 tbsp pure yuzu juice or lemon juice
1 tsp yuzu-kosho (yuzu and green chilli pepper paste), or more to taste
300 g (10½ oz) salmon fillet, cut into 2–3 pieces
200 g (7 oz/1 cup) quinoa, rinsed
360 ml (12 fl oz/1½ cups) Shojin Dashi (page 233) or your choice of stock
2 tbsp sake
1 tbsp extra virgin olive oil
1 garlic clove, minced
100 g (3½ oz) shimeji mushrooms, trimmed
4–5 cavolo nero leaves (Italian kale), cut into bite-size pieces
1 tbsp shoyu (or tamari for gluten free)
sea salt and freshly ground black pepper, to taste

Cooking quinoa in a donabe makes it surprisingly fluffy and flavourful, with a delicate nutty texture. It's so versatile that I often make a batch just to toss into salads. For this dish, I cook salmon and quinoa together in the donabe, then finish with sautéed kale and shimeji mushrooms. Everything is gently seasoned with a mix of yuzu-kosho (yuzu and green chilli pepper paste) and pure yuzu juice. It's a great one-pot meal packed with delicious flavour and balanced nourishment.

It is said that salmon warms the stomach and boosts circulation, quinoa supports energy and digestion, and kale helps gently detox and clear internal heat. It's also believed to be full of antioxidants – this is the kind of dish I love to nourish my body and support healthy skin from within.

EQUIPMENT: Classic-style donabe (or heavy duty pot) (1.2 litre/40 fl oz)

METHOD: Whisk together the yuzu juice and yuzu-kosho in a small bowl. Adjust the amount of yuzu-kosho according to your liking.

Season the salmon with ½ teaspoon sea salt and refrigerate for 30 minutes, then pat dry with paper towel.

Combine the quinoa, dashi and sake in a donabe. Cover and set over a medium-high heat. Once it comes to the boil, reduce to a low simmer and cook for 10 minutes, or until all the moisture has been absorbed.

About 1 minute before turning off the heat, place the salmon fillets on top of the quinoa. Let it rest for 10 minutes and let the salmon cook in the residual heat.

Meanwhile, heat the olive oil in a sauté pan over a medium heat. Add the garlic and sauté until aromatic, then add the shimeji mushrooms and cook for 2–3 minutes. Add the cavolo nero and continue sautéing until just wilted. Pour the shoyu around the edge of the pan and let it sizzle for another minute. Turn off the heat.

Uncover the donabe and gently break up the salmon. Fluff together with the quinoa using a large spoon. Add the cavolo nero mixture and yuzu-kosho mixture. Fluff again to combine. Taste and adjust the seasoning with salt and black pepper.

Ebi Nira Harusame

SIMMERED GLASS NOODLES WITH SPICY PRAWNS AND GARLIC CHIVES

海老韮春雨

Serves: 2–3

220 g (8 oz) prawns (shrimp), peeled and deveined
¼ tsp sea salt
3 tbsp sake
½ tbsp katakuriko (potato starch)
1 tbsp sesame oil
½ tbsp minced fresh root ginger
3-4 mini (bell) peppers (or ½ pepper), sliced
100 g (3½ oz) shimeji mushrooms, trimmed
½ tsp tobanjan (Chinese chilli bean paste)
300 ml (10 fl oz/1¼ cups) Awase Dashi (page 233) or your choice of stock
1 tbsp shoyu (or tamari for gluten free)
1 tbsp fish sauce
2 tbsp mirin
100 g (3½ oz) mung bean glass noodles, cut shorter if needed
60 g (2 oz) garlic chives, cut into 5 cm (2 in) lengths
sliced dried chilli, to taste (optional)
freshly ground black pepper, to taste
kurozu (Japanese black vinegar), to taste

Bold and spicy, this is a deeply warming one-pot dish of prawns (shrimp), garlic chives and harusame (Japanese glass noodles). I like using mung bean glass noodles for their smooth, elastic texture – especially the kind already cut into convenient lengths. They can go straight into the broth without soaking first, so they absorb all the flavour as they cook. The broth is seasoned with tobanjan (Chinese chilli bean paste), shoyu and fish sauce for extra depth. You can adjust the heat level by using more or less tobanjan. Garlic chives cook fast and go great with prawns, but you can use whatever vegetables you have on hand.

Prawns and garlic chives are said to be a classic combo for keeping the body warm, promoting blood flow and supporting core energy. This dish helps me stay active and balanced during the cold season.

EQUIPMENT: Classic-style donabe (or heavy duty pot) (1.2 litre/40 fl oz)

METHOD: Combine the prawns with the salt, 1 tablespoon of the sake and the katakuriko. Mix well.

Heat the sesame oil in a donabe over a medium heat. Add the ginger and sauté for about 1 minute until aromatic, then add the pepper and mushrooms and sauté for 1–2 minutes.

Push the vegetables to one side of the donabe and add the tobanjan to the empty space. Stir for about 30 seconds until aromatic, then mix everything together.

Add the remaining 2 tablespoons of sake to deglaze, then add the dashi, shoyu, fish sauce and mirin. Cover with the lid and bring back to a simmer, then add the glass noodles. Cover again and let the noodles soften and cook halfway, about 2 minutes.

Add the prawns and garlic chives, cover again and cook for 2–3 minutes, or until the noodles have absorbed most of the broth and everything is cooked through. Give it a gentle stir a couple of times as it cooks.

Sprinkle with sliced dried chilli, if using, then season with black pepper and a splash of kurozu to serve.

Kawara Soba

SIZZLING STEAM-FRIED MATCHA SOBA

瓦蕎麦

Serves 2–3

- 200 g (7 oz) matcha soba noodles or your choice of soba (see Note)
- ½ tsp katakuriko (potato starch)
- 1 tsp water
- 2 large eggs
- pinch of sea salt
- 2 tbsp extra virgin olive oil, plus extra for greasing the pan
- 2 garlic cloves, thinly sliced
- 150 g (5½ oz) shimeji mushrooms, trimmed
- 2 tbsp sake
- 5 g (¼ oz) dried mixed seaweed, rehydrated
- 220 g (8 oz) smoked salmon, sliced
- 3 tbsp shoyu (or tamari for gluten free)
- 1½ tbsp mirin

Colourful, fun and always delicious, this dish is inspired by kawara soba, a regional speciality from Yamaguchi Prefecture in western Japan, where matcha soba noodles are cooked and served sizzling on a heated *kawara* (roof tile). At home, I love making it in my tagine-style donabe, with its thick frying pan (skillet) base that keeps the noodles hot and lightly steamed while crisping the bottom just enough. It's seasoned simply – just a splash of sake, followed by shoyu and mirin to finish. They sizzle and lightly caramelise when added, enhancing the flavour even more. Topped with mixed seaweed, shredded egg crêpes and smoked salmon, the dish is beautiful to the eyes and even more enjoyable on the palate. You can easily switch up the ingredients cooked with the soba or used as toppings, depending on what you have. It's such a versatile dish.

EQUIPMENT: Tagine-style donabe (or frying pan/skillet with a lid)

METHOD: Bring a saucepan of water to the boil. Add the soba noodles and cook for about 2 minutes less than the package directions. Rinse under cold running water and drain well.

Thoroughly stir together the katakuriko and teaspoon of water in a bowl, then add the eggs and salt. Beat well.

Heat a medium sauté pan over a medium heat and lightly oil the surface. Pour in half of the egg mixture and tilt the pan to spread evenly. Once the surface is just set, gently flip and turn off the heat. Transfer to a cutting board. Repeat with the remaining egg. Stack the crêpes, slice in half, then roll into a log and cut into thin ribbons.

Add the 2 tablespoons of olive oil, garlic and mushrooms to the donabe. Sauté over a medium-high heat for about 2 minutes, then deglaze with the sake. Add the soba and spread evenly over the bottom, cover with the lid and steam-fry for 2–3 minutes.

Uncover and arrange the mixed seaweed, shredded egg crêpes and smoked salmon on top. Combine the shoyu and mirin, and pour around the edge of the donabe. Turn off the heat and let it sizzle.

Serve at the table.

NOTE: Matcha soba usually contain wheat flour. For a gluten-free option, use juwari (100 per cent buckwheat) soba.

FLAVOUR VARIATIONS: For a vegan version, omit the eggs and smoked salmon, and add plant-based ingredients. I like sautéing cavolo nero leaves with the mushrooms. Adding mixed herbs or grated nagaimo (mountain yam) for a topping is also nice. For non-vegetarian, you can also substitute the smoked salmon with other seafood or even seasoned sautéed minced (ground) meat.

Kani Asparagus Gohan

CRAB AND ASPARAGUS RICE
蟹とアスパラガス
の炊き込みご飯

Serves 4–5

2 Japanese rice cups (360 ml/12 fl oz/1½ cups) short-grain white rice, rinsed
320 ml (11¼ fl oz/1⅓ cups) Awase Dashi (page 233) or your choice of stock
2 tbsp sake
2 tbsp ayu (sweetfish) fish sauce or shoyu
100 g (3½ oz) enoki mushrooms, trimmed and cut in half
120 g (4 oz) Dungeness crab meat or other high-quality crab meat
100 g (3½ oz) medium-thick asparagus, woody ends trimmed, cut into 5 mm (¼ in) pieces and tips preserved
40 g (1½ oz) ikura (salmon roe) (optional)

Crab and rice always feel like such a treat to me, and this simple donabe recipe lets the natural sweetness of the crab shine. I add enoki mushrooms for a light, buttery accent and season the rice with ayu (sweetfish) fish sauce, which brings gentle umami without overpowering the crab. I love using fresh Dungeness crab when it's in season – it has such a clean, sweet flavour. A good alternative is high-quality crab meat (often sold in a tub) from a trusted fishmonger. To finish, I toss in asparagus, which steams gently in the donabe's residual heat and adds a crisp-tender texture.

Crab is thought to help support blood nourishment, while asparagus promotes gentle detoxification and aids digestion. This dish may help refresh the body and support clear, healthy skin from within.

EQUIPMENT: Double-lid donabe rice cooker (or heavy duty pot)

METHOD: Combine the rice, dashi, sake and fish sauce in a donabe. Let the rice soak for 20 minutes.

Evenly layer the enoki mushrooms and crab meat on top. Cover the donabe with both lids and cook over a medium-high heat for 13–15 minutes, or until 2–3 minutes after the steam starts puffing out of the top lid. (If cooking with a classic-style donabe or other pot, see Basic Rice Cooking Methods on page 170.)

Turn off the heat and let it rest for 15 minutes.

Quickly open the lids, add the asparagus and spread evenly over the rice. Cover again and let it rest for another 5 minutes.

Uncover and fluff gently with a rice paddle. Serve in individual bowls and top with a spoonful of ikura, if desired.

Soboro Oyako Don

CHICKEN AND EGG RICE
そぼろ親子丼

Serves 2

100 ml (3½ fl oz/scant ½ cup) Awase Dashi (page 233) or your choice of stock
2 tbsp sake
2 tbsp mirin
3 tbsp shoyu (or tamari for gluten free)
1 tsp katakuriko (potato starch)
220 g (8 oz) minced (ground) chicken (higher fat content preferred)
½ tbsp finely julienned fresh root ginger
3–4 shiitake mushrooms, trimmed and thinly sliced
5 large eggs
good pinch of sea salt

To serve

Plain White Rice (page 170), freshly cooked
Finely shaved katsuobushi (bonito flakes) (optional)
chopped mitsuba (Japanese parsley) or spring onion (scallion)
ground sansho (Japanese mountain pepper) or ichimi togarashi (ground red chilli pepper)

One of the most beloved Japanese donburi dishes, oyako don gets its name from *oyako* (parent and child) and *don* (short for *donburi*, or rice bowl), as the dish brings together chicken and egg. Instead of the traditional sliced chicken thigh, I actually prefer this version made with minced (ground) chicken. The texture is delicate and the soft eggs blend beautifully with the chicken and mushrooms. I like to serve with a generous sprinkle of good-quality katsuobushi (bonito flakes) over the rice before scooping the chicken and egg mixture on top – it creates such a magical combination of flavours. The toppings are flexible, but I usually go with mitsuba (Japanese parsley) and sansho (Japanese mountain pepper) for egg dishes, or a pinch of yuzu-flavoured chilli pepper for a nice aromatic kick. Shichimi togarashi, pickled ginger or your favourite herbs also work well.

Chicken and egg are both excellent sources of protein that are believed to help build *qi* (vital energy), making this dish great for both physical and mental recovery. Ginger and shiitake are thought to support digestion and gently warm the body. It's a nourishing bowl for a good recharge.

EQUIPMENT: Classic-style donabe (or heavy duty pot) (800 ml/27 fl oz)

METHOD: Combine the dashi, sake, mirin, shoyu, katakuriko and chicken in a donabe and stir well with chopsticks. Set over a medium heat and bring to a simmer, stirring often so the chicken stays soft and doesn't clump. Add the ginger and mushrooms, cover and continue to simmer for 4–5 minutes, or until the broth is slightly reduced and thickened.

Beat the eggs with a pinch of salt. Pour about two-thirds of the eggs evenly over the surface of the ingredients in the donabe. Cook for 45–60 seconds, or until the egg is just beginning to set. Pour in the remaining eggs, cover and cook for another minute. Turn off the heat and let rest for 2–3 minutes, or until the egg is cooked to your desired doneness.

To serve, scoop rice into each bowl and sprinkle a handful of katsuobushi on top, if using. Spoon the chicken and egg mixture over the top and garnish with mitsuba or spring onion. Enjoy with sansho, ichimi togarashi, or your favourite condiments.

Ninjin Wakame Gohan

CARROT AND WAKAME RICE
人参わかめご飯

Serves 4–5

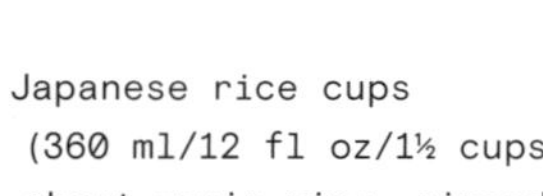

2 Japanese rice cups (360 ml/12 fl oz/1½ cups) short-grain rice, rinsed
350 ml (12 fl oz/1½ cups) Awase Dashi (page 233) or water
2 tbsp sake
1 tsp sea salt
180 g (6½ oz) carrot, finely julienned into 2.5 cm (1 in) lengths
5 g (about 2 tbsp) dried cut wakame seaweed, rehydrated and chopped
1 tbsp tamari
1 tsp pure yuzu juice or Meyer lemon juice
2 tbsp toasted white sesame seeds

Carrot is often treated as a sidekick, but this dish brings out the best in this humble ingredient – and I just can't get enough. A generous amount of finely shredded carrot is cooked with rice in minimal seasoning, and I'm amazed every time by how much flavour and natural sweetness it draws out. The tender carrot melds beautifully with wakame and crunchy toasted sesame seeds, and a hint of aromatic yuzu adds a bright, refreshing finish. I love enjoying this warm or at room temperature, especially as onigiri (rice balls). It's a favourite for picnics, too.

EQUIPMENT: Double-lid donabe rice cooker (or heavy duty pot)

METHOD: Combine the rice, dashi, sake and salt in a donabe. Let the rice soak for 20 minutes.

Add the carrot and spread evenly over the rice. Cover the donabe with both lids and cook over a medium-high heat for 13–15 minutes, or until 2–3 minutes after the steam starts puffing out of the top lid. (If cooking with a classic-style donabe or other pot, see Basic Rice Cooking Methods on page 170.)

Turn off the heat and let it rest for 20 minutes.

Meanwhile, mix the wakame, tamari and yuzu juice in a small bowl.

Remove the lids, add the wakame mixture and sesame seeds to the rice, and gently fluff thoroughly with a rice paddle.

NOTE: This dish pairs well with roasted seafood, grilled meat or a hearty vegetable salad.

Tamago-Gayu

EGG PORRIDGE
卵粥

Serves 1–2

500 ml (17 fl oz/generous 2 cups) water
½ Japanese rice cup (90 ml/3 fl oz/6 tbsp) short-grain white rice, rinsed
2 eggs
your choice of condiments (such as yuzu salt or nori furikake), to serve

Packed with childhood nostalgia and still one of my most frequently made dishes, this simple donabe egg porridge is made with just rice, water and egg, but it holds a special place in my heart. When I was little and not feeling well, my mom would make this for me and bring it to my bed in a small donabe. I always looked forward to it (so I kind of looked forward to getting sick!). It's so gentle on the stomach and easy to digest. Back then, I enjoyed it with just a sprinkle of table salt, but you can enjoy with different toppings or condiments, if you like. I often make it when I need to reset after too many dinners out or just crave something simple and good, with a little sea salt, yuzu salt or a sprinkle of nori furikake.

EQUIPMENT: Classic-style donabe (or heavy duty pot) (800 ml/27 fl oz)

METHOD: Bring the water to the boil in a donabe over a medium-high heat. Add the rice then reduce the heat to medium-low. Stir with a wooden spatula to make sure the rice isn't sticking to the bottom. Cover with the lid and slide it slightly open and simmer gently (the surface of the mixture should bubble quietly and steadily) for about 15–18 minutes, or until the porridge is smooth and slightly thickened.

Beat the eggs and drizzle into the donabe. Cover again and turn off the heat. Let it rest for 1–2 minutes, or until the egg is cooked to your desired doneness.

Serve in individual bowls and enjoy with your choice of condiments.

Touchi Tori Okowa

FERMENTED BLACK BEAN CHICKEN RICE
豆豉鶏おこわ

Serves 4–5

For the touchi marinade

2 tbsp touchi (Chinese fermented black beans), coarsely minced
1 garlic clove, minced
½ tbsp minced fresh root ginger
2 tbsp Shaoxing rice wine or sake
1 tsp tamari
1 tbsp oyster sauce
¼ tsp Chinese five spice powder
½ tbsp katakuriko (potato starch)
1 tbsp toasted sesame oil
1 tsp sliced dried chilli

For the chicken rice

220 g (8 oz) skinless, boneless chicken thighs, cut into medium bite-size pieces
1 Japanese rice cup (180 ml/ 6 fl oz/¾ cup) short-grain white rice, rinsed
1 Japanese rice cup (180 ml/ 6 fl oz/¾ cup) glutinous (sweet) rice, rinsed
2 tbsp multigrain mix (optional)
330 ml (11¼ fl oz/1⅓ cups) Tori Dashi (page 236) or your choice of stock, plus additional 2 tbsp if using multi-grain mix
3–4 shiitake mushrooms, trimmed and thinly sliced
60 g (2 oz) peeled roast chestnuts (see Note)
minced chives, to garnish

Juicy chicken marinated in savoury touchi (fermented black bean) sauce makes this dish deeply flavourful and comforting. I love how the dining space fills with a delicious aroma when I open the donabe lids. *Okowa* typically refers to a sweet rice dish, but here I use a mix of short-grain and glutinous (sweet) rice, so it's just perfectly chewy without feeling too heavy. I also like to add mixed grains for extra texture and nourishment, although that part is optional.

Touchi, ginger and shiitake are said to help warm the body and support digestion, which can ease tension and restlessness. It is thought that chicken nourishes *qi* (vital energy) and supports recovery from fatigue, while chestnuts gently soothe the stomach and promote relaxation. This dish helps me feel settled and warm – just right for a good night's sleep.

EQUIPMENT: Double-lid donabe rice cooker (or heavy duty pot)

METHOD: Whisk together the marinade ingredients. Add the chicken and mix well. Let marinate for 30 minutes to a few hours.

Combine both types of rice and the multigrain mix, if using, with the dashi in a donabe. Let the rice soak for 30 minutes.

Spread the chicken with the marinade evenly over the rice. Add the mushrooms and chestnuts between the chicken pieces. Cover the donabe with both lids and cook over a medium-high heat for 13–15 minutes, or until 2–3 minutes after the steam starts puffing out of the top lid. (If cooking with a classic-style donabe or other pot, see Basic Rice Cooking Methods on page 170.)

Turn off the heat and let it rest for 20 minutes.

Uncover and fluff gently with a rice paddle. Garnish with minced chives.

NOTE: Also called sweet chestnuts, you can find peeled roast chestnuts in packages at Asian markets or some grocery stores. They add just the right softness and mellow sweetness to this dish – and they're a nice source of fibre, too. You can also use peeled fresh chestnuts instead, when in season.

Orange Saffron Rice

BAKED ORANGE SAFFRON RICE
オレンジサフランライス

Serves 4–5

For the saffron rice

- pinch of saffron threads
- 2 tbsp hot water
- 2 tbsp extra virgin olive oil
- 2 garlic cloves, minced
- 1 shallot, minced
- 1 tsp cumin seeds
- 2 Japanese rice cups (360 ml/12 fl oz/1½ cups) basmati rice, rinsed
- 2 tbsp sake
- 2 bay leaves
- 1 tsp sea salt
- 480 ml (16 fl oz/2 cups) vegetable stock or your choice of stock

Toppings

- 2 tbsp unsalted butter
- 35 g (1¼ oz/¼ cup) shelled pistachios
- 30 g (1 oz/¼ cup) sultanas (golden raisins)
- 1 naval orange, zest peeled into strips and finely julienned (reserve the fruit or juice for another use)
- 2 tbsp white sesame seeds
- ½ tsp ground sansho (Japanese mountain pepper)
- chopped dill, to garnish

This fragrant baked rice is full of colour, texture and warming spices. Cooking basmati rice in a donabe requires less liquid than usual, resulting in light, fluffy grains with a gently crisped bottom – and the rice stays hot for a long time. The saffron rice is topped with a sautéed mix of pistachios, sultanas (golden raisins), orange peel and sesame seeds, then finished with fresh dill and a touch of sansho (Japanese mountain pepper) for a bright, uplifting aroma. It's festive but simple, perfect on its own or as a beautiful side for gatherings. I especially love pairing it with a curry, like Nanohana Curry (page 86).

EQUIPMENT: Double-lid donabe rice cooker (or heavy duty pot)

METHOD: Preheat the oven to 220°C/425°F (200°C/390°F fan).

Put the saffron threads in a small cup and pour over the hot water. Let infuse for 15–30 minutes before starting to cook the dish.

Heat the olive oil in a donabe over a medium heat. Add the garlic, shallot and cumin seeds, and sauté for a couple of minutes until aromatic. Add the basmati rice and stir to coat, then add the sake, bay leaves, salt and saffron with its infused water. Stir again. Add the stock and cover with both lids, increase the heat to medium-high and bring to a high simmer.

Transfer to the oven and bake for 20 minutes.

Remove from the oven and let rest, undisturbed, for 15 minutes.

Meanwhile, prepare the toppings. Heat the butter over a medium heat in a sauté pan. Add the pistachios, sultanas, orange peel and sesame seeds. Sauté for a few minutes until aromatic, then add the sansho and stir. Remove from the heat.

To finish, uncover both lids of the donabe and spread the toppings over the rice. Garnish with chopped dill and fluff with a rice paddle at the table to serve.

NOTE: Instead of vegetable stock, chicken stock also works very well for this dish. For a vegan version, replace the butter with more olive oil.

FLAVOUR VARIATIONS: Feel free to swap ingredients for the toppings – different kinds of dried fruits (such as cranberry or barberry), nuts (walnuts or pine nuts), or herbs (coriander/cilantro or parsley) can be fun to try.

Miso Nikomi Ramen

MISO-SIMMERED RAMEN
味噌煮込みラーメン

Serves 2

For the miso broth

4 tbsp white miso (not the sweet kind like Saikyo miso)
1 tbsp sesame paste or tahini
2 tbsp sake
750 ml (25 fl oz/3 cups) Shojin Dashi (page 233) or your choice of stock

For the toppings

½ corn-on-the-cob or about 100 g (3½ oz/½ cup) tinned sweetcorn (corn)
100 g (3½ oz) broccoli rabe (rapini)
4–5 g (¼ oz) cut dried wakame, rehydrated (about ½ cup soft)
1 tbsp unsalted butter (optional for plant-based), in two pieces
shredded pickled ginger, to taste
ground toasted white sesame seeds, to taste
la-yu (chilli oil), to taste

For the donabe

1 tbsp sesame oil
2 garlic cloves, thinly sliced
2 servings (150–200 g/5½–7 oz) dried instant ramen (see Note)

It's often easy to feel heavy or even a little tired after a bowl of rich ramen – but this dashi-based miso ramen is rich, packed with flavour and leaves me feeling good and energised every time. Toppings of corn and butter are a classic match I love for miso ramen, and I like to add wakame and broccoli rabe (yes, greens!) for extra texture and a tender bitterness that balances the richness. The broth is gently infused with garlic, and the miso is blended with a touch of sesame paste for lingering depth. There's a wide variety of instant ramen noodles available, including gluten-free and even colourful, healthier options. It's fun to explore and find the ones you like to cook with. A favourite of mine is brown rice and millet ramen.

EQUIPMENT: Classic-style donabe (or heavy duty pot) (1.2 litre/40 fl oz)

METHOD: To make the broth base, whisk together the white miso, sesame paste and sake in a bowl. Gradually whisk in the dashi until smooth.

Separately blanch the sweetcorn, if using fresh, and broccoli rabe in boiling water (about 5 minutes for the sweetcorn and 2 minutes for the broccoli rabe). If using a donabe steamer (recommended), steam the sweetcorn for 3 minutes, then add the broccoli rabe and continue to steam for 2 more minutes. Let cool slightly, then slice the kernels off the cob and cut the broccoli rabe into 5 cm (2 in) lengths.

Heat the sesame oil in a donabe over a medium-low heat, add the garlic and sauté for 1–2 minutes until fragrant. Add the miso broth, increase the heat to medium-high and bring to a high simmer. Add the ramen and cook for 1–2 minutes until the noodles start to loosen. Cover, remove from the heat and let rest for 1–2 minutes until the noodles are al dente.

Uncover, arrange the toppings over the noodles and let the butter melt. Serve immediately.

NOTE: If you are using non-instant ramen (dry or soft), par-boil the noodles separately before adding to the broth. In that case, reduce the dashi by about 200 ml (7 fl oz/scant 1 cup), since the noodles won't absorb as much liquid.

FLAVOUR VARIATION: You can enjoy this with seafood, meat (including leftovers) or any other toppings you like. I sometimes add sliced prosciutto, too!

VII

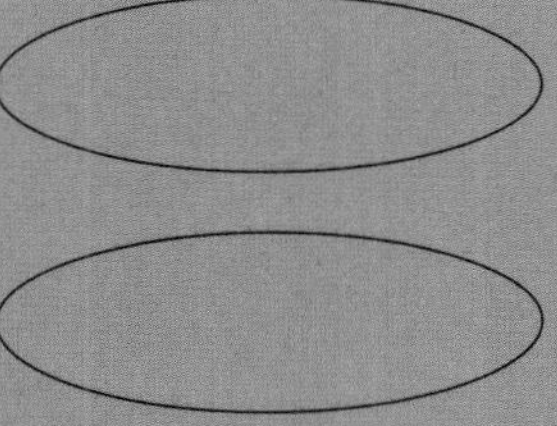

WAGASHI SWEETS

I've loved making sweets since I was a young child. One of my earliest memories is picking wild mugwort leaves around the neighbourhood and making kusa mochi (mugwort mochi dumplings) with my mom in the spring. The fresh green aroma and sweet anko filling are still vivid to me. Some recipes in this chapter are classic-style wakagashi (traditional Japanese confections), while others blend wagashi elements with Western flavours. A few are prepared in a donabe, which always makes the process feel more special. Many are just mildly sweet, which I find more satisfying. Although the recipes call for different sugars, I often use sugar-free natural sweeteners instead of regular sugar, since I like to minimise my sugar intake. My favourites are erythritol or a monk fruit and allulose blend, which comes in both white and brown varieties and lets you appreciate the sweets and still feel good, without compromising flavour or texture.

Mizu Yokan

COLD SWEET ADZUKI JELLY
水羊羹

Makes 1 mould
(about 6–8 servings)

- 420 ml (14 fl oz/1¾ cups) water
- 4 g (¼ oz) kanten (agar) powder
- 2 tbsp Okinawa black sugar or raw brown sugar
- 500 g (1 lb 2 oz) Anko (page 221)
- ¼ tsp sea salt

Mizu yokan is a popular summer wagashi and one of the easiest traditional Japanese desserts to make. It's a cold jelly made with Anko (page 221), water and kanten (agar), and tastes especially refreshing on hot days. I make it often during the summer. It's so smooth and light, I usually end up eating two slices – or more – at a time. You can use either homemade anko or a good-quality store-bought kind – koshian (smooth) or tsubuan (coarse) both work. I use a rectangular mould with a removable tray to make unmoulding and slicing easier. You can also use individual size cups in different shapes.

EQUIPMENT: Rectangular mould (with a removable inner tray) (15 x 13.5 x 4 cm/6 x 5½ x 1¾ in) or similar-size mould

---

METHOD: Combine the water and kanten powder in a saucepan. Set over a medium heat and bring to the boil, then reduce the heat to low and simmer gently for 1–2 minutes.

Add the sugar, and the anko in three additions, stirring well each time to fully incorporate. Once the mixture is smooth and starts to gently simmer again, add the salt and turn off the heat. Let it cool slightly, about 10–15 minutes, and stir again to ensure avoiding separation, then pour into the mould.

Refrigerate until fully set and chilled (about 2 hours). Carefully lift the tray and turn it over to unmould, and slice to serve.

NOTES: You can adjust the amount of sugar to add according to your liking.

Mizu yokan keeps well in the refrigerator for up to 2 days.

Matcha Madeleine

I love anything matcha, whether it's in drinks, savoury dishes or sweets. This is one of my most repeated matcha recipes, and I've been making it for many years. Instead of using traditional shell moulds, I bake the whole batter in a donabe. It turns out wonderfully every time. The donabe's thick clay body distributes heat evenly, giving the cake a gently caramelised edge and a moist, buttery interior. I enjoy tasting it while it's still warm, just as much as after it's cooled. And if you can wait, after a couple of days the flavour and texture settle nicely, and it tastes even better.

MATCHA MADELEINE
抹茶マドレーヌ

Serves 6–8

- 70 g (2½ oz/generous ⅓ cup) rice flour (see Note)
- 30 g (1 oz/generous ¼ cup) ground almonds (almond flour)
- 1 tsp baking powder
- ½ tsp sea salt
- 1 tbsp matcha powder
- 130 g (4½ oz/1 stick plus 1 tbsp) unsalted butter, sliced
- 90 g (3¼ oz/generous ⅓ cup) pure cane sugar
- 2 large eggs, at room temperature

EQUIPMENT: Classic-style donabe (or heavy duty pot) (1.2 litre/40 fl oz)

METHOD: Preheat the oven to 180°C/350°F (160°C/320°F fan). Line the bottom of a donabe with baking parchment.

Sift together the rice flour, ground almonds, baking powder, salt and matcha.

Melt the butter in a small pan over a low heat.

Whisk together the sugar and eggs in a mixing bowl until smooth. Add the flour mixture in three additions, whisking after each addition. Whisk in the melted butter.

Pour the batter into the donabe and bake, uncovered, for about 35 minutes, or until a skewer inserted in the centre comes out clean.

Let cool in the donabe for 15–30 minutes before unmoulding.

NOTE: Rice flour gives the cake just the right soft density, but you can make it with plain (all-purpose) flour, too.

Kokuto Miso Mushi-Pan

MISO AND OKINAWA BLACK SUGAR STEAMED CAKE

黒糖味噌蒸しパン

Makes 1 mould (about 6–8 servings)

- 0 g (2 oz/½ cup) plain (all-purpose) flour (see Note)
- 0 g (1½ oz/generous ⅓ cup) ground almonds (almond flour)
- tsp baking powder
- 0 g (1½ oz) unsalted butter, sliced
- 0 g (1¾ oz/generous ¼ cup) Okinawa black sugar or substitute raw brown sugar
- large egg
- generous tbsp miso (aged brown rice or red miso is preferred)
- tbsp double (heavy) cream or milk (or your choice of plant-based milk)

This simple donabe-steamed cake is made with miso and Okinawa black sugar for a deep, almost minerally sweetness and gentle umami. The texture is soft and surprisingly light – and I love the small patches where the dark sugar melts into little spots. I use a blend of plain (all-purpose) flour and ground almonds (almond flour) for a moist, tender crumb, but you can use only plain flour if you prefer.

EQUIPMENT: Donabe steamer (or pot with a steam basket) (3 litre/100 fl oz or larger), rectangular mould (with a removable inner tray) (15 x 13.5 x 4 cm/6 x 5½ x 1¾ in) or similar-sized heatproof tin (pan)

METHOD: In a large bowl, sift together the plain flour, ground almonds and baking powder.

Put the butter in a small pan and melt over a low heat.

Whisk together the sugar and egg in a bowl until smooth. Add the miso, melted butter and cream or milk one at a time, whisking well after each addition.

Add the dry mixture in 2–3 batches, mixing gently with a spatula each time until combined.

Line the mould with baking parchment, then pour the batter into the mould.

Set up the donabe steamer and bring the water to the boil. Place the mould inside and steam over a medium-high heat for about 17 minutes, or until a skewer inserted in the centre comes out clean.

NOTE: For a gluten-free version, you can substitute the plain flour with a gluten-free baking flour blend or rice flour. The texture will be a bit denser with a soft chew.

FLAVOUR VARIATION: Add some small cubed satsumaimo (Japanese sweet potatoes) – they go especially well with the miso and black sugar.

Matcha Shio-Koji Cookies

MATCHA SHIO-KOJI COOKIES
抹茶塩麹クッキー

Makes about
20 small cookie balls

VG GF

120 g (4 oz/generous ⅔ cup) rice flour
80 g (2¾ oz/¾ cup) ground almonds (almond flour)
50 g (1¾ oz/¼ cup) pure cane sugar
1 tbsp matcha powder, sifted
120 ml (4 fl oz/½ cup) coconut oil (see Flavour Variation)
4 tsp Shio-Koji (page 238)
4 tsp plain almond milk or your choice of milk
4 tbsp pine nuts
icing (powdered) sugar, for dusting

These gently sweet cookies combine the earthy richness of matcha with the subtle umami of shio-koji. Pine nuts add a soft crunch and nutty aroma, and the final dusting of icing (powdered) sugar makes them feel just a little extra special. This recipe is so simple – just mix the dough by hand in a bowl, shape into balls and bake. The rice flour gives them a light, crisp texture, but you can also use plain (all-purpose) wheat flour if you don't need them to be gluten-free. I love making these for tea time or as a small homemade gift in a box.

METHOD: Preheat the oven to 165°C/330°F (145°C/290°F fan). Line a baking sheet with baking parchment.

In a large bowl, whisk together the rice flour, ground almonds, sugar and matcha. Add the coconut oil, shio-koji and almond milk, and mix by hand until a soft dough forms. Mix in the pine nuts.

Form into 2 cm (¾ in) balls and arrange on the baking sheet, leaving space between each for expansion. Bake for 15–18 minutes, or until just firm to the touch.

Let cool completely, then sift icing sugar over the top.

FLAVOUR VARIATION: Try using extra virgin olive oil instead of coconut oil. I love the way it brings out both the matcha and the grassy notes of the oil.

Sake-Kasu Pound Cake

The naturally sweet aroma and elegant flavour of sake fill this rich, buttery cake. I like to use fresh, high-quality sake-kasu (sake lees) – the softer kind works especially well. If yours is firm, you can blend it with a little sake to make a smooth paste. It's hard to resist while still warm, but the flavour and texture get even better after a day or two of rest. The alcohol from the sake-kasu is cooked off, but if you're very sensitive, please keep that in mind.

SAKE-KASU POUND CAKE
酒粕パウンドケーキ

Makes 1 loaf cake

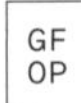

50 g (1¾ oz/½ cup) walnuts
65 g (2¼ oz/generous ½ cup) plain (all-purpose) flour (see Note)
35 g (1¼ oz/⅓ cup) ground almonds (almond flour)
1 tsp baking powder
125 g (4½ oz/1 stick plus 1 tbsp) unsalted butter, at room temperature
90 g (3¼ oz/scant ½ cup) raw brown sugar
50 g (1¾ oz) sake-kasu (sake lees) (softer kind preferred), at room temperature
2 large eggs, at room temperature

EQUIPMENT: 10 x 20 cm (4 x 8 in) loaf tin (pan)

METHOD: Preheat the oven to 180°C/350°F (160°C/320°F fan). Line the bottom of the loaf tin (pan) with baking parchment.

Spread the walnuts on a baking sheet and roast for 7–8 minutes, or until lightly golden and fragrant. Let cool, then break into small pieces.

In a large bowl, sift together the plain flour, ground almonds and baking powder.

In a stand mixer fitted with the whisk attachment, whisk the butter until smooth. Add the raw brown sugar and continue mixing until fluffy. Add the sake-kasu and mix again until fully combined.

In a separate bowl, beat the eggs. Gradually add the eggs to the butter mixture in about 10 additions, mixing as you go.

Remove the bowl from the mixer and fold in the flour mixture in three batches using a spatula. Fold in the roasted walnuts.

Pour the batter into the prepared loaf tin and bake for about 40 minutes, or until a skewer inserted in the centre comes out clean. About 15 minutes into baking, remove the loaf and score the surface lengthwise with a knife (this helps it to rise evenly and creates a clean split on top). Return it to the oven.

Let cool for at least 15 minutes and gently remove from the loaf tin. Slice to serve.

NOTE: For a gluten-free version, you can substitute the plain flour with a gluten-free baking flour blend or rice flour. The texture may be slightly more delicate with rice flour, but it still works well.

FLAVOUR VARIATION: Adding small dried fruit like raisins, blackcurrants or candied citrus peel is also nice – they complement the sake-kasu's gentle sweetness and add a pleasant bite.

Hojicha Chocolate Ice Cream

HOJICHA CHOCOLATE ICE CREAM

焙じ茶チョコレート
アイスクリーム

Makes about 800 ml (27 fl oz/scant 3½ cups)

1 tbsp kudzu starch or arrowroot starch
180 ml (6 fl oz/¾ cup) almond milk or your choice of plant-based milk
60 ml (2 fl oz/¼ cup) mirin
100 g (3½ oz/½ cup) raw brown sugar
1 x 400 g (14 oz) can coconut cream
3 tbsp cocoa powder
1 tbsp hojicha (roasted green tea, loose leaf)

This all-plant-based ice cream is rich and creamy, just the way I like it. The combination of gently infused smoky hojicha (roasted green tea) and cocoa is unexpectedly delicious and comforting. The mixture is gently thickened with kudzu starch, and mirin adds subtle complexity. Be sure to use hon-mirin (genuine fermented mirin) for the best results.

EQUIPMENT: Ice-cream maker

METHOD: Whisk the kudzu starch and almond milk in a saucepan until smooth. Add the remaining ingredients and whisk over medium-low heat. Bring to a low simmer over moderate heat then gently simmer for 1–2 minutes to steep the tea.

Remove from the heat and strain through a fine-mesh sieve (strainer) into a bowl. Let cool, then chill completely in the refrigerator for several hours or overnight.

Transfer to an ice-cream maker and churn according to the manufacturer's instructions.

NOTES: Homemade ice cream is best eaten within a week or so. If it becomes too firm in the freezer, just let it sit at room temperature until soft enough to scoop.

For a zero-calorie sugar alternative, most sweeteners (including erythritol) tend to freeze very hard, so I don't recommend them. If a monkfruit and allulose blend, or allulose alone, is available in your area, that's what I suggest using. If using allulose on its own, increase the amount to 130 g (4½ oz). Allulose helps prevent the ice cream from turning rock-hard by lowering the freezing point more effectively than regular sugar. That way, you can enjoy a rich and creamy texture, even after freezing.

Matcha Ice Cream

This is a variation of my plant-based ice cream. Smooth and rich, with deep, intense matcha flavour. Make sure to use a high-quality ceremonial-grade matcha for the best results.

MATCHA ICE CREAM
抹茶アイスクリーム

Makes about 800 ml (27 fl oz/scant 3½ cups)

- 1½ tbsp matcha powder, sifted
- 3 tbsp hot water
- 1 tbsp kudzu starch or arrowroot starch
- 180 ml (6 fl oz/¾ cup) almond milk or your choice of plant-based milk
- 100 g (3½ oz/½ cup) pure cane sugar
- 60 ml (2 fl oz/¼ cup) mirin
- 1 x 400 g (14 oz) can coconut cream

EQUIPMENT: Ice-cream maker

METHOD: Whisk together the matcha and hot water in a small bowl.

Whisk the kudzu starch and almond milk in a saucepan until smooth. Add the remaining ingredients and whisk over a medium-low heat. Bring to a low simmer over moderate heat then simmer for 1–2 minutes.

Remove from the heat. Whisk a few ladlefuls of the mixture into the matcha, one at a time, then stir it back into the pot. Strain through a fine-mesh sieve (strainer) into a bowl. Let cool, then chill completely in the refrigerator for several hours or overnight.

Transfer to an ice-cream maker and churn according to the manufacturer's instructions.

Ninjin Yuzu Jam Muffin

CARROT AND YUZU MARMALADE MUFFIN

人参とゆずジャムのマフィン

Makes 2 small cakes (about 4–6 servings)

GF OP

- 60 g (2 oz/½ cup) plain (all-purpose) flour (see Note)
- 60 g (2 oz/generous ½ cup) ground almonds (almond flour)
- 1 generous tsp baking powder
- ½ tsp sea salt
- 1 tsp ground cinnamon
- 30 g (1 oz/scant ⅓ cup) walnuts
- 1 large egg, at room temperature
- 60 g (2 oz/⅓ cup) plus 1 tsp raw brown sugar
- 60 g (2 oz) yuzu marmalade or orange marmalade
- 60 ml (2 fl oz/¼ cup) extra virgin olive oil
- 120 g (4 oz) carrot, coarsely grated
- ½ tbsp candied yuzu or citrus peels (optional)

I've been making these large muffin cakes for years, and every time I give one to someone as a gift, I always get asked for the recipe. The combination of grated carrot and yuzu marmalade gives it gentle sweetness, light citrus notes and beautiful moisture. Ground almonds (almond flour) keeps the texture tender and the cinnamon sugar topping brings a gentle spiced finish. I like to play around with different variations – sometimes I use courgette (zucchini) instead of carrot, or swap the marmalade for blueberry jam. I usually bake the batter in two small donabe egg bakers or heatproof glass pots, but a small loaf pan or ramekins work just as well.

EQUIPMENT: 2 donabe egg bakers/glass pots/ramekins (about 12–13 cm/ 4¾–5 in in diameter) or a small loaf tin (pan) lined with baking parchment

---

METHOD: Preheat the oven to 180°C/350°F (160°C/320°F fan). Line the mould with baking parchment.

Sift the plain flour, ground almonds, baking powder, salt and cinnamon into a large bowl.

Spread the walnuts on a small baking sheet and roast in the oven for 7–8 minutes, or until lightly golden and fragrant. Let cool, then chop.

In a separate bowl, whisk together the egg, the 60 g (2 oz/⅓ cup) of sugar, marmalade and olive oil until smooth. Add the grated carrot and stir to combine.

Fold in the flour mixture in three additions, mixing gently with a spatula each time. Add the walnuts and fold in.

Pour the batter into the prepared pots or pan and sprinkle the candied citrus peels (if using) and the teaspoon of sugar over the top. Bake for 40–45 minutes, or until a skewer inserted in the centre comes out clean.

Let cool, then remove from the mould/s. Slice and serve.

NOTE: For a gluten-free version, you can substitute the plain flour with a gluten-free baking flour blend or rice flour. The texture may be slightly denser but still moist and delicious.

Anko

SWEET ADZUKI BEAN PASTE
あんこ

Makes about 750 ml (25 fl oz/3 cups)

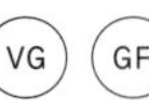 

- 300 g (10½ oz) dried adzuki beans, rinsed
- water, as needed
- 200 g (7 oz/generous 1 cup) raw brown sugar
- 30 g (1 oz/2 tbsp plus 2 tsp) Okinawa black sugar or extra raw brown sugar
- ⅓ tsp sea salt

The culture of wagashi, or Japanese confectionery, can't be explained without anko. Loved in Japan for hundreds of years, anko is enjoyed on its own or used in many traditional sweets. While it's easy to buy pre-made anko, I find most commercial versions too sweet. Making it from scratch in a donabe is simple, and the result tastes so much more precious. My version is gently sweet, and a little Okinawa black sugar adds depth and richness to the flavour. I often substitute the raw brown sugar with a monkfruit and allulose blend sweetener, but I like to keep the Okinawa black sugar for its nice depth.

Adzuki beans are thought to be a powerhouse when it comes to gently clearing the body. Believed to support digestion, reduce puffiness and help release excess moisture, just a small amount may support the body's natural rhythm and help your overall balance.

EQUIPMENT: Classic-style donabe (or heavy duty pot) (1.8 litre/60 fl oz or larger)

METHOD: Combine the adzuki beans and about 1 litre (34 fl oz/4¼ cups) water in a large saucepan. Set over a medium-high heat and bring to the boil, then reduce the heat and simmer for about 3 minutes.

Drain and rinse the beans in warm water (this removes bitterness and helps them cook with a cleaner, more pleasant flavour). Drain again.

Transfer the parboiled beans to the donabe and add about 800 ml (27 fl oz/scant 3½ cups) water.

Cover and set over a medium-high heat. Bring to the boil, then reduce the heat to a gentle simmer. Simmer for 1–1½ hours until the beans are very tender. Cooking time and how quickly water is reduced vary depending on the type of adzuki and vessel (thicker-body donabe tend to need less water and cook faster).

Check and stir a few times after 30 minutes, and add more water, as needed. The beans should be barely covered with liquid when they are ready. If there is too much liquid at this stage, ladle out the excess.

Add both sugars and increase the heat to medium-high. Stir for about 5 minutes to dissolve the sugar and start glazing the beans.

Add the salt and reduce the heat to low. Continue simmering until the beans are glossy and thickened to a soft paste, about 5–10 minutes.

Remove from the heat and let cool. The anko will thicken further as it cools.

Serve on its own or use as a filling or topping for desserts. You can store anko in the refrigerator for 4–5 days or freeze it for up to 1 month.

Shiratama An

ANKO WITH PURPLE SWEET POTATO SHIRATAMA

白玉あん

Serves 2–3

VG GF

- 90 g (3¼ oz/½ cup) shiratamako (glutinous rice flour)
- 10 g (½ oz) pure purple sweet potato powder
- 100 ml (3½ fl oz/scant ½ cup) water, or as needed
- Anko (page 221), to serve

Serving anko with mochi or shiratama balls is a simple and delightful way to enjoy it as a dessert. Shiratama is a type of mochi dumpling made from shiratamako, a kind of glutinous rice flour. It's quick to make, and its bouncy texture is hard to resist. Here, I mix in purple sweet potato powder for its vibrant colour and delicate flavour. You can serve it with plain shiratama, or the tofu shiratama used in the Tofu Shiratama Miso-Shiru recipe (page 82) can work beautifully, too.

METHOD: To make the shiratama dumplings, mix the shiratamako, purple sweet potato powder and water in a bowl, and knead well by hand. If the mixture feels a bit dry, add more water, a little at a time. Knead until the texture is soft but not wet – almost like play-dough. Roll into 12 balls by hand.

Bring a large saucepan of water to the boil and add the balls. Once they float, about 2 minutes, boil for 30 seconds or a little longer. Meanwhile, prepare a bowl of cold water. Transfer the cooked dumplings to the cold-water bath to cool, then drain well.

Divide into small bowls and top with anko to serve.

NOTE: Shiratama are best served fresh, but you can refrigerate leftovers in water for up to 1 day. If they are firm, reheat briefly in hot water before serving.

FLAVOUR VARIATION: Additional toppings like kinako (roasted soybean flour) and a drizzle of kuromitsu (brown sugar syrup) or maple syrup are great, too.

Matcha Tiramisu

MATCHA TIRAMISU
抹茶ティラミス

Serves 3–4

For the matcha cream

120 ml (4 fl oz/½ cup) double (heavy) cream, chilled
pinch of sea salt
4 tbsp pure cane sugar, divided
1 tbsp matcha powder, sifted
240 ml (8 fl oz/1 cup) coconut yoghurt or Greek-style yoghurt

For the matcha brew

200 ml (7 fl oz/scant 1 cup) hot water
1½ tbsp matcha powder, sifted

To assemble

120 ml (4 fl oz/½ cup) Anko (page 221), or more as needed
6 or more sponge fingers (ladyfingers) (wheat or gluten-free kind)
extra matcha powder, for dusting

This is a tiramisu for serious matcha lovers. Every bite is rich with deep matcha flavour, balanced by the gentle bitterness that pairs beautifully with the anko (sweet adzuki bean paste) at the bottom. I use coconut yoghurt for the cream base, because I love its flavour and it gives a clean finish. I fold in just enough whipped cream to add a little richness. It's my kind of guiltless tiramisu, with the real 'lift me up' quality that the name tiramisu is meant to suggest. It's a flexible dessert and I use different vessels depending on the occasion – sometimes small individual cups, other times a large dish to share. Either way, it always feels special.

EQUIPMENT: 12–13 cm (4¾–5 in) diameter x 7 cm (3 in) high round bento box or similar-size dish

METHOD: To make the matcha cream, whip the cream, salt and 2 tablespoons of the sugar in a bowl until stiff peaks form.

In a spearate bowl, whisk together the matcha and remaining 2 tablespoons of sugar. Add the yoghurt in three additions, whisking until smooth after each addition. Gradually add the whipped cream and whisk until well blended. Keep chilled.

To make the matcha brew, pour the hot water over the matcha in a bowl and whisk well.

To assemble the tiramisu, spread the anko in the bottom of the bento box or a serving dish in a flat, thin layer. Quickly dip both sides of the sponge fingers in the matcha brew, one at a time, and place over the anko in a single layer. Cover with some matcha cream. Make another layer of soaked sponge fingers and matcha cream. Depending on the size of your serving dish, you may have some leftover ingredients. Cover and chill for at least 1 hour, or up to overnight.

Sift the matcha directly over the surface and serve.

NOTE: For a vegan option, use plant-based whipping cream instead of dairy cream, and vegan sponge fingers or sponge cake.

FLAVOUR VARIATION: For a caffeine-free version, use mulberry matcha. Made from powdered mulberry leaves, it has a naturally sweet flavour and no caffeine. It's very kid-friendly, too. You can enjoy it for drinking or use it in cooking just like green tea matcha.

Ukishima

STEAMED SWEET ADZUKI BEAN CAKE

浮島

Makes 1 mould
(about 6–8 servings)

- 200 g (7 oz) Anko (page 221), or use store-bought koshian, smooth sweet adzuki bean paste, for a finer texture)
- 2 large eggs, separated
- 2 tbsp almond milk or your choice of milk
- 1 tbsp rice flour or plain (all-purpose) flour
- 2 tbsp raw brown sugar
- ¼ tsp sea salt
- 50 g (1¾ oz) dried dates, chopped

Ukishima is a traditional Japanese steamed cake made with anko (usually koshian, or smooth sweet adzuki bean paste) and gently folded meringue. The name means 'floating island', and the texture is as light as it sounds – moist, soft and just sweet enough. I make it with my own Anko (page 221), which adds more body and depth, but you can use store-purchased koshian if you prefer a finer texture. It's called a cake, but only a small amount of rice flour is used to hold everything together. It makes a lovely dessert, especially with a bowl of fine matcha.

EQUIPMENT: Donabe steamer (or pot with a steam basket) (3 litre/100 fl oz or larger), rectangular mould (with a removable inner tray) (15 x 13.5 x 4 cm/6 x 5½ x 1¾ in) or similar-sized heatproof tin (pan)

METHOD: Line the mould with baking parchment.

In a large bowl, whisk the anko and egg yolks until smooth. Add the milk and flour one at a time, whisking until smooth after each addition.

In a separate bowl, beat the egg whites with a pinch of the sugar and the salt. When they begin to foam, add the remaining sugar and continue beating until stiff peaks form.

Add a scoop of the meringue into the anko mixture and mix to loosen, then gently fold in the remaining meringue in two more additions until just combined.

Fold in the chopped dates, then pour the batter into the mould.

Set up the donabe steamer and bring the water to the boil. Place the mould in the steamer and steam over a medium heat for about 25 minutes, or until a skewer inserted into the centre comes out clean.

Remove from the heat and let cool slightly in the mould, then refrigerate until fully chilled.

Unmould and slice to serve.

NOTE: *Ukishima* keeps well in the refrigerator for up to 3–4 days.

FLAVOUR VARIATION: Try chopped roasted chestnuts instead of dates. They add a nice nutty flavour.

VIII

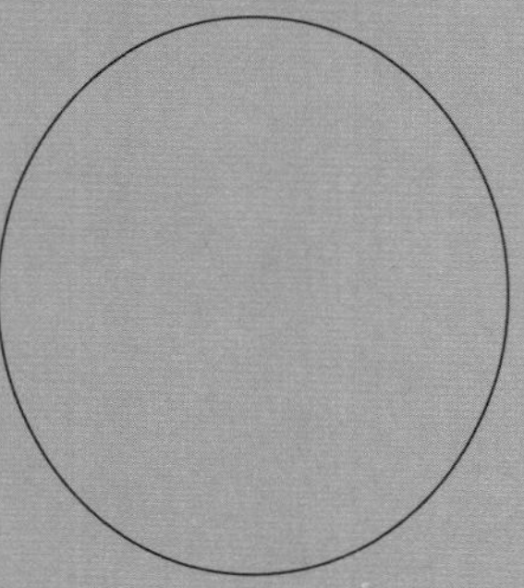

DASHI, SAUCES & CONDIMENTS

It's no secret that savoury dashi, flavourful sauces and versatile condiments form the foundation of my everyday cooking. These essentials not only bring depth and umami to dishes, but they also make cooking simpler and more fun. Even the most basic ingredients can turn into something special when paired with the right sauce or a well-made dashi. Today, life can feel easier with so many kinds of pre-made products available, but I find that making your own dashi from scratch, fermenting your own condiments, or whisking up a quick sauce can help you slow down, bring quiet focus and sharpen your senses through the rhythm of daily cooking. I think that's more rewarding. These homemade staples are not only delicious but also offer nutritional benefits and help support a more well-balanced lifestyle.

Dashi Basics

Dashi is the foundation of Japanese cuisine. I believe it's thanks to this unique and elegant umami that the Japanese 'art of subtraction' philosophy exists. Sometimes, I just want to taste the dashi on its own with minimal seasoning to enjoy its soothing effect. Other times, it becomes the quiet backbone of a dish – never standing out, but gently bringing all the flavours into balance. I'm always amazed by how many roles dashi can play. Making it in a donabe brings out the best of each ingredient through gentle, even heat.

Here, I introduce my two basic dashi: Awase Dashi and Shojin Dashi. These are the dashi I rely on for many dishes in this book, and I always feel a little calmer just making them, even on a busy day.

MAIN INGREDIENTS FOR MY DASHI

KOMBU: A dried kelp rich in natural umami. I usually use thick Ma-kombu or Rishiri kombu from Hokkaido. Store in a cool, dry place and wipe gently to remove any dust before use. There is no need to rinse off the white powder, as it's a naturally occurring umami component formed during the drying process.

KATSUOBUSHI: Smoked and dried bonito (skipjack tuna), sold either as a block or pre-shaved in various sizes. I use hanakatsuo, the larger flake type, for a clean, aromatic broth. Once opened, store it in a tightly sealed bag in the refrigerator.

DRIED SHIITAKE MUSHROOMS: Once rehydrated, they have a meaty texture and rich aroma. Choose ones with thick, rounded caps for better flavour. Store in a cool, dry place.

STOVE-TOP INFUSION METHODS

Awase Dashi

The clean umami from kombu and the round, smoky depth of bonito creates a perfect balance to this dashi that's both delicate and deeply flavourful.

KOMBU AND BONITO DASHI
合わせ出汁

Makes about 1 litre (34 fl oz/4¼ cups)

10–15 g (⅓–½ oz) kombu (dry kelp; about 2–3 pieces, 10 x 10 cm/4 x 4 in)
1.2 litres (40 fl oz/5 cups) water (low mineral content preferred)
15 g (½ oz) katsuobushi (bonito flakes)

METHOD: Soak the kombu in the water in a bowl for 2–3 hours, or at least 30 minutes.

Transfer the kombu and water to a donabe and set over a medium heat, uncovered. Just before the water starts boiling, about 25–30 minutes, remove the kombu.

Increase the heat to medium-high, then as soon as the water starts boiling, turn off the heat and add the katsuobushi all at once. Let sit for about 2 minutes until the katsuobushi settles to the bottom.

Strain through a fine-mesh sieve (strainer) into a bowl. The dashi is ready to use.

Shojin Dashi

This is a standard dashi used in traditional shojin ryori (Buddhist temple cuisine). Dried shiitake gives the broth a rich, pronounced flavour, while kombu offers a cleaner, more soothing umami. You can adjust the ratio of the two depending on the dish. A deeper shiitake flavour works well for stews and braised dishes, while lighter soups benefit from more kombu and less shiitake for a more delicate finish.

KOMBU AND SHIITAKE MUSHROOM DASHI
精進出汁

Makes about 1 litre (34 fl oz/4¼ cups)

10 g (⅓ oz) dried shiitake mushrooms (about 4 small-medium pieces)
10–15 g (⅓–½ oz) kombu (dry kelp; about 2–3 pieces, 10 x 10 cm/4 x 4 in)
1.2 litres (40 fl oz/5 cups) water (low mineral content preferred)

EQUIPMENT: Classic-style donabe (or heavy duty pot) (1.8 litre/60 fl oz)

METHOD: Quickly rinse the shiitake mushrooms under running water.

Soak the kombu and shiitake in the water in a bowl for 2–3 hours, or until the shiitake are fully rehydrated.

Transfer the kombu, shiitake and their soaking water to a donabe and set over a medium heat, uncovered. Just before the water starts boiling, about 25–30 minutes, remove the kombu and shiitake, squeezing the excess liquid out of the shiitake into the broth. The dashi is ready to use.

直火不可
HARIO

Other Really Easy Ways to Make Delicious Dashi and Other Tips

Here are some of my favourite tips and everyday methods for making dashi, plus how I like to use leftover ingredients.

COLD INFUSION METHOD

I often make a large batch the night before. Cold infusion creates a clean, pure-tasting dashi with no effort. Just soak the ingredients in water and refrigerate overnight (or for at least 6 hours), then strain. It's ready to use.

HOT 'POUR-OVER' INFUSION METHOD

This is another method I use often, especially on busy weekdays. It's convenient because I can make just the amount I need, whether that's a small bowlful for a single serving or a larger batch, without having to watch the heat or time it closely. The result is always a beautifully balanced dashi, ready to go.

Boil water and pour it over the ingredients in a bowl. Let it steep for 10–15 minutes for Awase Dashi or 15–30 minutes for Shojin Dashi, then strain. You can infuse longer if you like. I usually prepare it at the start of meal prep and let it sit until I'm ready to use it.

VARIATIONS AND WATER-TO-INGREDIENT RATIO

You can use kombu, katsuobushi or shiitake on their own – or combine them in any way you like. Since I make dashi so often, I rarely measure and just eyeball the ingredients. As a general guideline, use about 1.5–3 per cent of the total water weight in dashi ingredients. That's roughly 15–30 g (½–1 oz) of ingredients per 1 litre (34 fl oz/4¼ cups) water, depending on how strong you want the flavour to be.

READY-MADE DASHI BAGS

When I need quick dashi, I also love using high-quality store-bought dashi bags. You can find versions for both awase dashi and shojin-style plant-based dashi. Be sure to choose a kind that contains only the natural ingredients you'd use for homemade dashi. Some cheaper versions may use lower-quality ingredients, which can result in a duller or less clean flavour. I also like opening the bag and using the contents as a seasoning for soups, sautéed or simmered dishes, dressings, or even adding to water to cook flavoured rice.

STORING DASHI

For me, the fresher the better when it comes to dashi. I usually make just enough to use within a couple of days. Once made, it keeps for 2–3 days in the refrigerator or up to a month in the freezer. I never freeze my dashi, but if you plan to freeze it, I recommend using ice-cube trays, so you can easily take out just the amount you need.

LEFTOVER INGREDIENTS

After making dashi, the leftover ingredients don't need to go to waste. Shiitake mushrooms can be sliced (stems removed) and added to soups, cooked with rice, or used in simmered dishes. Kombu can be reused in stocks or simmered in shoyu and mirin to make tsukudani – a savoury-sweet condiment often eaten with rice. Katsuobushi can be sautéed with sesame seeds and other seasonings to make a simple homemade furikake.

Tori Dashi

JAPANESE CHICKEN STOCK
鶏出汁

Makes about 1 litre (34 fl oz/4¼ cups)

GF

600 g (1 lb 5 oz) chicken wings
1 tsp sea salt
1.2 litres (40 fl oz/5 cups) water
240 ml (8 fl oz/1 cup) sake
one 10 x 10 cm (4 x 4 in) piece kombu (dry kelp)
2 spring onions (scallion) (green part only)
1 garlic clove, peeled and left whole
1 small knob fresh root ginger, sliced
6 black peppercorns

This isn't a traditional Japanese stock, but it's a soup base I use often for a wide variety of dishes, including Chinese-inspired meals. I find chicken wings make the most flavourful stock, thanks to all the collagen-rich bones and skin. The flavour is deep yet clean, and it can be enjoyed on its own with just a pinch of salt – or turned into a simple, comforting ramen with a splash of shoyu. Leftover chicken can be used for salad, soup or rice bowls.

EQUIPMENT: Classic-style donabe (or heavy duty pot) (1.8 litre/60 fl oz)

METHOD: Season the chicken wings all over with the salt and let rest in the refrigerator for a few hours, or at least 30 minutes.

Combine the water, sake and kombu in a donabe and let soak for 30 minutes.

Pat the chicken wings dry with paper towel and add to the donabe along with the spring onion tops, garlic, ginger and peppercorns. Set over a medium to medium-high heat. As soon as the liquid starts boiling, remove the kombu.

Reduce the heat to maintain a gentle simmer, skim the surface and cover with the lid. Simmer for 30–45 minutes.

Turn off the heat and let rest for 30 minutes–1 hour.

Strain. The dashi is ready to use.

Kombu Shoyu-Koji

FERMENTED RICE KOJI WITH SHOYU AND KELP

昆布醤油麹

Makes about 500 ml (17 fl oz/generous 2 cups)

- 180 g (6 oz/scant 1 cup) dried rice koji
- 320 ml (11 oz/scant 1⅓ cups) shoyu (or tamari for gluten free)
- 3 x 3 cm (1 x 1 in) piece of kombu (dry kelp) (about 4 g)

Along with Shio-Koji (page 238), shoyu-koji is a widely used homemade fermented seasoning in Japan. Like miso, both are probiotic-rich, containing beneficial living bacteria from the fermentation process. As you may know, shoyu is traditionally made by fermenting soybeans with rice koji, creating its signature deep umami. Shoyu-koji takes this a step further – essentially a double fermentation of shoyu – resulting in a wonderfully mellow, rounded flavour. I like to add a piece of kombu during fermentation, which enhances the umami even further. You can often replace shoyu with an equal amount of shoyu-koji in various dishes and may be surprised by how much depth it adds while reducing overall salt content. Commercial versions are also available if you don't have homemade shoyu-koji on hand.

METHOD: Massage the rice koji by hand in a bowl for 30–60 seconds, rubbing the grains against each other until slightly fragrant.

Transfer the mixture to a 1 litre (34 fl oz/4¼ cup) jar, or a large-enough jar that there is enough space for mixing, and add the shoyu, stirring gently to combine. Insert the kombu into the mixture, submerging it, then cover.

Keep the jar in a cool area, away from direct sunlight. Stir the mixture once a day to ensure even fermentation.

The shoyu-koji will be ready in 10–14 days. Once fermented, transfer to a smaller container, if preferred, and store it in the refrigerator. It will keep for a few months in a tightly sealed container.

NOTES: For a quick dipping sauce, mix equal parts kombu shoyu-koji and extra virgin olive oil.

Use kombu shoyu-koji straight as a marinade for vegetables, fish or meat for grilling or roasting. Mix with spices or other seasonings to create different flavour variations.

Shio-Koji

FERMENTED RICE KOJI WITH SALT

塩麹

Makes about 420 ml (14½ fl oz/1¾ cups)

180 g (6 oz/scant 1 cup) dried rice koji
60 g (2 oz/scant ½ cup) sea salt
180 ml (6 fl oz/¾ cup) water

One of the first workshops I ever hosted was on making shio-koji and Amazake (page 240) back in the late 2000s. I still remember how excited my guests were to discover just how easy shio-koji is to make – and how incredibly flavourful it is. This fermented seasoning is like an umami-packed version of salt, bringing depth and subtle sweetness to dishes. You can often replace salt with shio-koji at a ratio of 1 part salt to 3–4 parts shio-koji. Once you start using it, it quickly becomes a kitchen essential! Commercial versions are also available if you don't have homemade shio-koji on hand.

METHOD: Massage the rice koji by hand in a bowl for 30–60 seconds, rubbing the grains against each other until slightly fragrant.

Add the salt and continue rubbing for another 30–60 seconds until well incorporated and the mixture feels slightly sticky.

Transfer the mixture to a 1 litre (34 fl oz/4¼ cup) jar, or a large-enough jar that there is enough space for mixing, and add the water. Stir gently, then cover. Keep the jar in a cool area, away from direct sunlight. Stir the mixture once a day to ensure even fermentation.

The shio-koji will be ready in 10–14 days and the consistency will become like a thick porridge. Once fermented, transfer to a smaller container, if preferred, and store it in the refrigerator. It will keep for a few months in a tightly sealed container.

NOTES: For a quick dipping sauce, mix equal parts shio-koji and extra virgin olive oil.

Use shio-koji straight as a marinade for vegetables, fish or meat before grilling or roasting. Mix with spices or other seasonings to create different flavour variations.

Kaeshi

MULTIPURPOSE SHOYU-BASED UMAMI SAUCE

かえし

Makes about 450 ml (15 fl oz/scant 2 cups)

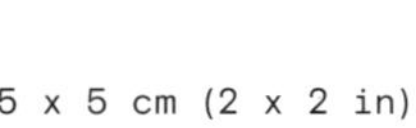

- one 5 x 5 cm (2 x 2 in) piece kombu (dry kelp)
- 2 dried shiitake mushrooms
- 120 ml (4 fl oz/½ cup) sake
- 150 ml (5 fl oz/scant ⅔ cup) mirin
- 2 tbsp Okinawa black sugar or raw brown sugar
- 240 ml (8 fl oz/1 cup) shoyu (or tamari for gluten free)

This is one of my essential seasoning bases – so versatile, just mildly sweet and deeply flavourful. I always keep a batch in my refrigerator to use in stir-fries, rice dishes, soups and as a dipping sauce for cold soba noodles when diluted with dashi or water (dilute in a 1:1 ratio). It's also great drizzled over cooked protein, chilled tofu, or even natto (fermented soy beans). With just a few simple ingredients, it's easy to make at home and has a wonderfully deep flavour. As a bonus, the shiitake used to make kaeshi becomes richly seasoned and delicious – I love slicing them up and mixing them into rice or salads.

METHOD: Combine all the ingredients in a saucepan and let the kombu and shiitake soak for 30 minutes.

Bring to a simmer over medium heat, then reduce the heat to medium-low and gently simmer for about 5 minutes, reducing by 15–20 per cent.

Turn off the heat and let it cool completely to further infuse the flavours before removing the kombu and shiitake. Use immediately, or cover and store in the refrigerator for up to 2 weeks.

Kaeshi Ponzu

QUICK PONZU SAUCE WITH KAESHI

かえしぽん酢

Makes as much as you need

- Kaeshi (see above)
- your choice of citrus (single or a combination of yuzu, sudachi, lemon, grapefruit, lime, etc.), juiced

I introduced different kinds of homemade ponzu in my last book, *DONABE*. I like them all, but this one is the easiest to make as long as you have kaeshi on hand. You can mix it up instantly whenever you need it. This is an extremely flexible recipe – simply adjust the ratio of kaeshi and citrus to suit your taste.

METHOD: Mix the kaeshi and citrus juice at a standard ratio of 2:1 to 1:1, depending on your preference.

NOTE: Mix the kaeshi ponzu with some finely diced fresh tomatoes for a refreshing topping for grilled fish or steak.

Amazake

SWEET FERMENTED RICE
甘酒

Makes about 900 ml
(30 fl oz/scant 4 cups)

1 Japanese rice cup (180 ml/ 6 fl oz/¾ cup) glutinous (sweet) rice, rinsed
600 ml (20 fl oz/2½ cups) water, or more as needed
200 g (7 oz/1 cup) rice koji

Often called 'drinking IV' in Japan for its nutrient-rich properties, amazake is a traditional fermented drink prized for its ability to help fight fatigue and support overall well-being. Made from just sweet rice and rice koji, it naturally develops a mild sweetness as the enzymes break down starches into sugars. Amazake can be enjoyed on its own, diluted with water to drink, blended into smoothies, or incorporated as a natural sweetener – offering a more nourishing alternative to refined sugar, while adding depth and flavour to both savoury and dessert dishes. I personally love mixing it into yoghurt for a nourishing start to the day. A small serving is often enough to enjoy its rich, satisfying flavour. Commercial versions are also available if you don't have homemade amazake on hand.

EQUIPMENT: Classic-style donabe (or heavy duty pot) (1.5 litre/50 fl oz), yoghurt maker

---

METHOD: Combine the rice and water in a donabe. Let the rice soak for 30 minutes.

Cover and set over a medium heat. Gradually bring to the boil, about 15–20 minutes, then reduce the heat to a low simmer. Continue to cook for about 15 minutes, stirring often, until the rice turns into a very soft porridge. If it thickens too much before fully softening, add more water as needed to prevent burning.

Turn off the heat and let it stand for 45 minutes, or until the temperature cools to between 70–75°C (158–167°F).

Massage the rice koji by rubbing the grains against each other with one hand for 1–2 minutes until fragrant – this helps activate the koji. Stir the rice koji into the porridge, mixing thoroughly with a spatula.

Transfer the mixture to a yoghurt maker and set it to 65°C (149°F). Let it ferment for 11 hours.

Transfer to a blender (I like using my Vitamix) and blend for about 10 seconds, or until smooth.

Amazake can be stored in the refrigerator for 3–5 days, or for 3–4 weeks in the freezer.

Amazake Goma Miso Tare

AMAZAKE SESAME MISO SAUCE
甘酒胡麻味噌たれ

Makes about 100 ml (3½ fl oz/scant ½ cup)

- 3 tbsp toasted white sesame seeds, ground
- 1 tbsp miso (I prefer white miso)
- 3 tbsp Amazake (see opposite)
- 1 tbsp rice vinegar
- 1 tsp shoyu (or tamari for gluten free)

This probiotic-rich sauce combines the natural sweetness of amazake with the deep, savoury flavour of miso. I love using it as a pour-over sauce for vegetables like in steamed eggplant (page 50) or as a dip for crudités.

METHOD: Whisk together all the ingredients until smooth.

Use immediately or store in the refrigerator for up to 2 days.

Kurumi Miso

WALNUT MISO CREAM
胡桃味噌

Makes about 120 ml (4 fl oz/½ cup)

- 40 g (1½ oz/generous ⅓ cup) walnuts
- tbsp miso
- 1 tsp maple syrup
- 1 tbsp rice vinegar
- water or dashi, as needed (optional)

Kurumi miso has rich roasted walnut flavours, deep miso notes and a subtle tang from rice vinegar. I love mixing it with green beans (page 41) or pairing it with all kinds of vegetables. It's also one of my favourite toppings or fillings for onigiri (rice balls). When I want to use it as a sauce to pour over dishes, I just thin it out with a little water or dashi.

METHOD: Preheat the oven to 180°C/350°F (160°C/320°F fan).

Spread the walnuts on a baking sheet and roast for 7–8 minutes, or until lightly golden and fragrant.

Combine all the ingredients in a food processor and process until smooth. Adjust the consistency by adding a small amount of water or dashi, if desired. You can leave some small chunks of walnuts for texture or process until very fine, whichever you prefer. Alternatively, grinding the mixture in a mortar and pestle creates a lovely rustic texture.

Use immediately or store in the refrigerator for up to 2 days.

Goma Almond Butter Sauce

SESAME ALMOND BUTTER SAUCE

胡麻アーモンドバターソース

Makes about 120 ml (4 fl oz/½ cup)

1 garlic clove, skin on (optional)
3 tbsp toasted white sesame seeds
2 tbsp almond butter
½ tbsp raw brown sugar
1 tsp shoyu (or tamari for gluten free)
1 tbsp rice vinegar
½ tbsp or more Shio-Koji (page 238)

This creamy sauce brings together the deep, nutty flavours of sesame and almond, making it a perfect match for potatoes, including sweet potatoes (see Murasaki-Imo, Goma Almond Butter Sauce-Ae, page 44), as well as grilled or roasted vegetables. I love adding roasted garlic for an extra layer of richness, but you can skip it for a milder flavour.

METHOD: Preheat the oven to 200°C/400°F (180°C/350°F fan).

If using, roast the garlic, skin on, until soft, about 10 minutes. Let it cool slightly, then peel.

Grind the sesame seeds in a mortar and pestle to your desired consistency. Add the roasted garlic and pound well to incorporate.

Add the remaining ingredients and grind until smooth. Adjust the seasoning with more shio-koji, if needed. If a smoother consistency is preferred, stir in a small amount of water.

Use immediately or store in the refrigerator for up to 2 days.

Shira-Ae Koromo

TOFU CREAM FOR SHIRA-AE

白和え衣

Makes about 240 ml (8 fl oz/1 cup)

300 g (10½ oz) medium-firm tofu
1 tbsp or more Shio-Koji (page 238)

Vegetables coated in silky tofu cream are a staple in *shojin ryori* (Buddhist temple cuisine) and a popular home dish in Japan. In this version, the ingredients are simply tofu and shio-koji, and I love how this cream highlights the natural flavour of whatever it is paired with. In addition to Corn Shira-Ae (page 47), I also enjoy it with a variety of vegetables or fruits, such as spinach, persimmon, kabocha squash, and more.

METHOD: Place the tofu in a shallow tray and top with a flat tray or small cutting board. Add a weight 1–1.5 times the tofu's weight and let it sit for 30 minutes to remove excess moisture. Drain the liquid and pat the tofu dry with a paper towel.

Combine the tofu and shio-koji in a food processor and process until smooth. Add more shio-koji if desired to adjust the seasoning. Alternatively if you prefer, grinding the mixture in a mortar and pestle creates a lovely rustic texture.

Use immediately or store in the refrigerator for up to 1 day.

FLAVOUR VARIATION: For an extra layer of umami, try adding a touch of Saikyo miso.

Shoga Miso Dressing

GINGER MISO VINAIGRETTE
生姜味噌ドレッシング

Makes about 120 ml
(4 fl oz/½ cup)

- 2 tbsp miso
- 1 tbsp raw brown sugar
- 1 tsp finely grated fresh root ginger
- 1 garlic clove, minced
- 1 tbsp lemon juice
- 2 tbsp rice vinegar
- 1 tbsp sesame oil
- 2½ tbsp extra virgin olive oil
- ½ tbsp toasted white sesame seeds

Ginger and miso are always a great combination, and this vinaigrette brings together their bright, zesty flavour and deep umami richness. It's versatile – perfect for tossing with fresh vegetables such as in Ruccola Salad (page 58) or as a refreshing dressing for cold soba noodles.

METHOD: Whisk together the miso, sugar, ginger, garlic, lemon juice and vinegar in a bowl.

Slowly whisk in the sesame oil, followed by the olive oil until fully emulsified. Stir in the sesame seeds.

Use immediately or store in the refrigerator for up to 2 days.

Shio-Koji Dressing

SHIO-KOJI VINAIGRETTE
塩麹ドレッシング

Makes about 100 ml
(3½ fl oz/scant ½ cup)

- ½ tsp finely grated garlic
- ½ tsp finely grated fresh root ginger
- 1 tbsp finely minced shallot
- 1 tsp Dijon mustard
- 1 tbsp Shio-Koji (page 238)
- 1 tsp usukuchi shoyu
- 2 tbsp rice vinegar
- ½ tbsp toasted sesame oil
- 60 ml (2 fl oz/¼ cup) extra virgin olive oil
- Freshly-ground black pepper, to taste

This Japanese-meets-French-style vinaigrette is light, bright and leaves a nice umami aftertaste. The gentle saltiness and natural sweetness of shio-koji make it a perfect match for crisp salads. I especially love it with my Daikon Salad (page 51) or drizzled over leafy greens with a boiled egg on top.

METHOD: Whisk together the garlic, ginger, shallot, mustard, shio-koji, usukuchi shoyu and rice vinegar in a bowl.

Gradually whisk in the sesame oil, followed by the olive oil until emulsified. Stir in black pepper to taste.

Use immediately or store in the refrigerator for up to 2 days.

NOTE: For a gluten-free option, substitute usukuchi shoyu with 1 tbsp or more shio-koji.

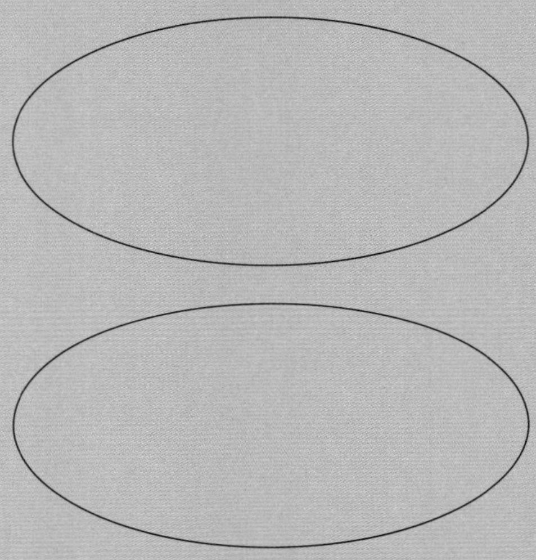

MENU IDEAS

MENU ONE

Plant-Based Small Dishes

A traditional Japanese meal consists of rice, miso soup, and a few small dishes – offering a simple, nourishing way to enjoy a balanced diet. Pictured on pages 48–49.

ZAKKOKU GOHAN

Plain White Rice with Multigrain Mix

page 170

TOFU SHIRATAMA MISO-SHIRU

Tofu Dumpling and Brussels Sprouts Miso Soup

page 82

CORN TOFU

Corn Kudzu Jelly Cake

page 46

SHOGA HIJIKI

Quick-Simmered Ginger Hijiki

page 59

MUSHI NASU, AMAZAKE GOMA MISO TARE

Steamed Aubergine with Amazake Sesame Miso Sauce

page 50

AKA CABBAGE SHIO-KOMBU SALAD

Red Cabbage and Shio-Kombu Salad

page 43

MENU TWO

A Summer Meal

One of my favourite kinds of summer meals to enjoy outside – light, vibrant, and easy to prep ahead. So many fun flavours with minimal effort. Pictured on pages 104–105.

HAKKO OTSUMAMI TRIO

Probiotic Small Bites with Fermented Flavours

page 42

CORN SHIRA-AE

Corn in Tofu Cream

page 47

KIKURAGE SALAD

Wood Ear Mushroom and Coriander Salad

page 54

MUSHI SALMON TO MAME SOUP

Steamed Black Garlic Salmon and Clams with Pea Soup

page 116

UME IWASHI TAKIKOMI GOHAN

Sardine and Pickled Plum Rice

page 175

MATCHA MADELEINE

Matcha Madeleine

page 208

MENU THREE

A Donburi Meal

A hearty and comforting donburi bowl for energy. Paired with pickles, miso soup and a veggie side, it makes a wholesome and satisfying weeknight meal. Pictured on pages 178–179.

SOBORO OYAKO DON

Chicken and Egg Rice

page 191

HAKUSAI ASA-ZUKE

Quick-Pickled Napa Cabbage in Shio-Koji

page 55

LENTIL DAIKON MISO-SHIRU

Lentil and Daikon Miso Soup

page 90

SAYAINGEN KURUMI MISO-AE

Green Beans in Walnut Miso Cream

page 41

MENU FOUR

Hotpot Gathering

Colourful, festive and delightful – a meal made for gathering around the table, where everyone can take part and create memories together. Pictured on pages 144–145.

GYU-MAKI WATERCRESS SHABU SHABU

Thinly Sliced Beef-Wrapped Watercress Hotpot

page 142

MUSHI-ZAKANA NO GOMA ABURA SAUCE

Steamed Halibut with Sizzling Sesame Oil Sauce

page 102

SATOIMO NO TOMO-AE

Taro in Taro Sauce

page 53

DAIKON SALAD, SHIO-KOJI DRESSING-AE

Daikon Salad with Shio-Koji Vinaigrette

page 51

NINJIN WAKAME GOHAN

Carrot and Wakame Rice

page 193

Let's Slow Down

Happiness and health go hand in hand. They are both precious – and never something to take for granted. I believe that health is the foundation of happiness. And for me, it's not about following a specific diet, but about creating a lifestyle that supports both. Even when I'm busy, I try to slow down and take a moment. I value quiet daily rituals: lighting incense, opening windows to let fresh *qi* (vital) energy flow through the home, brewing tea, sitting down to eat slowly. Happiness comes from within.

In Japanese culture, we say *itadakimasu* ('I humbly receive') before eating and *gochisosamadeshita* ('thank you for the meal') after. Whether I'm sharing food with someone or eating a simple meal on my own, I always say those words. They remind me to appreciate the moment, the ingredients and the life around me. Cooking with donabe has been one of these rituals. It slows me down, brings me back to myself and helps me focus on what matters.

Every day, donabe cooking inspires me to take care of myself – by choosing ingredients thoughtfully and paying attention to how I nourish my body. Hearing the gentle sound of simmering, watching the steam rise from the lid and the moment I lift the lid are all part of the joy. And whether I'm sharing a meal or eating alone, I feel grounded and grateful. People often tell me, 'I love watching you eat.' I take that as a beautiful compliment. Every bite is a joy.

In Japan, we have an old saying: *hara hachibu* – eating until you're about eighty per cent full. My mom used to remind me of this often. It's a key to both health and happiness. *Hara hachibu* is just enough. It helps you pay more attention, savour each bite more slowly and stay in balance – and it's sustainable. We don't need to be full to the brim to feel satisfied. A gentle, steady sense of happiness – just enough – is more than enough.

This book is not just a collection of recipes. It's my way of sharing the joy I've found through a donabe lifestyle – one slow meal, one happy moment at a time.

About the Author

Naoko Takei Moore is an acclaimed expert in donabe and Japanese home cooking, based in Los Angeles. She introduced donabe culture to the US, Europe and beyond at a time when it was virtually unknown outside Japan and other parts of Asia.

Originally from Tokyo, she graduated from Aoyama Gakuin University in Tokyo with a degree in International Politics, Economics, and Business. She began her career in the music industry and worked with several prominent UK artists before moving to Los Angeles to pursue a path in wine and culinary arts. She earned her Wine Expert Certification from the Japan Sommelier Association in 2000 and later developed wine programmes at Le Cordon Bleu in Los Angeles.

Naoko is the co-author of *Donabe: Classic and Modern Japanese Clay Pot Cooking* (Ten Speed Press, 2015) and author of *A Very Asian Guide to Japanese Food* (Gloo Books, 2024). She is the founder and owner of TOIRO, a West Hollywood shop and online store specialising in authentic donabe, Japanese kitchen tools and artisan tableware. Her company also serves as the official US representative of Nagatani-en, a revered donabe producer in Iga, Japan, since 1832.

Her passion for sharing the joy of donabe cooking continues through her writing, teaching and everyday meals. Her work has been featured in *The New York Times*, *Los Angeles Times*, and other major outlets. She also enjoys exploring fine teas.

TOIROKITCHEN.COM
INSTAGRAM: *@mrsdonabe*

Acknowledgements

I started with passion in 2008 – importing donabe and sharing donabe cooking in the US, even though almost no one around me knew what it was. I believed then, as I do now, that donabe is a language that connects people across cultures. With the support of those who opened their hearts with curiosity, donabe cooking has continued to grow in ways I never imagined. I'm grateful to be writing my second book about it.

Thank you to everyone who believed in me and walked this path with me – this book is for you.

EVE MARLEAU It all started with a short email from you. Thank you for giving me this special opportunity – and for bringing together such a wonderful team – to express my love for donabe cooking in a beautiful and meaningful way.

EILA PURVIS Thank you for guiding the project so thoughtfully from London, and for always bringing your energy and enthusiasm. Your encouragement meant so much and truly kept me going.

TEGAN ELLA HENDEL Your design captured the warmth and nuance I love. Thank you for making the book feel not only personal, but like something to be kept and cherished.

EMILY PREECE-MORRISON Thank you for editing this enormous amount of text – and for navigating Japanese, American and British expressions so skilfully.

BEE BERRIE Thank you for your talent and professionalism in making the shoot such a success – and for turning the hard days into fun ones. Your food styling and energy brought it all to life, Bee-san!

MATT RUSSELL Every photo you took felt magical – I was so excited each time I saw them. Thank you for capturing the personality and beauty of my happy donabe cooking, Oshaberi Matto-san!

RANDI BROOKMAN HARRIS Thank you for your thoughtful direction with the prop styling and for making each dish shine. I also loved spending time with you, going over every piece of tableware in my home.

BEN BARON, LILLIAN BERLINER, and JJ JENNIFER JENNER Thank you for cooking and bringing my recipes to life. Working with each of you in the kitchen was such a joy – and always full of excitement.

KAI GOURMET Thank you for generously providing all the seafood for the photoshoot (kaigourmet.com). Your incredibly fresh ingredients truly helped make the dishes shine.

LAKANTO Thank you for generously providing your natural monkfruit and allulose sweeteners (lakanto.com), so I could make delicious desserts – without the guilt!

STEVE SCALFATI You supported me through every step of this book-making journey. Thank you for always encouraging me – and even offering your space for the final days of the shoot.

Love,
Naoko

Index

Page refs in *italics* are illustrations

Quadrille, Penguin Random House UK, One Embassy Gardens, 8 Viaduct Gardens, London SW11 7BW

Quadrille Publishing Limited is part of the Penguin Random House group of companies whose addresses can be found at global.penguinrandomhouse.com

Published by Quadrille in 2026

www.penguin.co.uk

A CIP catalogue record for this book is available from the British Library

ISBN 978-1-83783-446-4
10 9 8 7 6 5 4 3 2 1

Managing Director, Publishing:
Sarah Lavelle

Publishing Director:
Kajal Mistry

Senior Commissioning Editor:
Eve Marleau

Senior Editor:
Eila Purvis

Designer:
Tegan Ella Hendel

Photographer:
Matt Russell

Props Stylist:
Randi Brookman Harris

Food Stylist:
Bee Berrie

Copy Editor:
Emily Preece-Morrison

Proofreader:
Sue Juby

Indexer:
Cathy Heath

Production Controller:
Martina Georgieva

Colour reproduction by p2d

Printed in China by C&C Offset Printing Co., Ltd.

The authorised representative in the EEA is Penguin Random House Ireland, Morrison Chambers, 32 Nassau Street, Dublin D02 YH68.

Penguin Random House is committed to a sustainable future for our business, our readers and our planet. This book is made from Forest Stewardship Council® certified paper